Edward Payson Hammond

Sketches of Palestine

Descriptive of the Visit of the Rev. Edward Payson Hammond...

Edward Payson Hammond

Sketches of Palestine
Descriptive of the Visit of the Rev. Edward Payson Hammond...

ISBN/EAN: 9783337013837

Printed in Europe, USA, Canada, Australia, Japan

Cover: Foto ©ninafisch / pixelio.de

More available books at **www.hansebooks.com**

Sketches of Palestine

DESCRIPTIVE OF THE VISIT

OF THE

REV. EDWARD PAYSON HAMMOND, M.A.

TO THE

HOLY LAND

WITH INTRODUCTION BY THE
REV. ROBERT KNOX, D.D.
Pastor, Linen Hall Street Presbyterian Church, Belfast

LONDON
MORGAN & CHASE, 38 LUDGATE HILL
NEW YORK:
T. NELSON & SONS, 52 BLEECKER STREET.
1869.

INTRODUCTION.

AN opportunity was given me of reading these 'Sketches' before they were sent to press. I read them with intense interest, and, I can add, with profit, and I feel confident that my experience will be that of thousands.

There are few subjects on which we have such a plethora of literature as Palestine, and yet this volume will be found fresh and striking, and to possess features of interest and excellence entirely its own. The gifted author has cast his observations and reflections into verse; and though it cannot be said that every part of the book is of equal merit, the appreciative reader will not fail very often to realize that he is in the presence of a man of power. In the description of some of the scenes, imperishably associated with the life and sufferings of our Lord, one feels that the heart of the author is in sympathy with the subject; all his spiritual force and fire are called forth, and the creations of his imagination indicate poetic genius of a high order.

Apart from their literary merit, these sketches will be highly valued by Christian readers, because of the fulness and frequency with which the precious Gospel is set forth. Bible lands are often visited by those who have no living faith in the Son of God. They are drawn there by other considerations than love to Him. How barren and meaningless must be their reflections compared with the man whose heart is full of adoring love to the Saviour!

What can the mere man of letters, or the antiquarian or sentimentalist, enjoy in a visit to Bethlehem, or Gethsemane, or Calvary, or the place where Jesus was laid, compared with the man who can say, and is not ashamed to say, 'He loved me, and gave Himself for me?'

The reader is not treated here to cold criticism on a point of disputed topography. The heart of the author is too much filled with love to Him whose footprints made all these places sacred to linger over such questions, and hence we find him, ever and anon, breaking forth in the language of prayer and praise, or commending to others the Saviour so dear to himself.

The name of the author is withheld; for what reason we are unable to discern. Few of those who have read Mr. Hammond's 'Jesus the Way,' published by the Sunday-School Union, or who are familiar with his 'Hymns of Salvation,' can fail to recognise the same loving heart and rich and fervid imagination, and especially the same tendency, in all things, and at all times, to speak of Him who is 'all our Salvation and all our Desire.'

None but those who are unacquainted with Mr. Hammond's history will think it strange that he should have held special meetings for children in Jerusalem and other cities of the East. From his early manhood he has taken an absorbing interest in the young—not in the way of promoting any system of mere education, but in directly seeking their *salvation*. To this work he has given so much of his time and energies that he is known as 'the Children's Friend,'—a high honour, and well merited. In America, in Canada, the British Isles, the Continent of Europe, and in the far distant lands of the Bible he has collected large numbers of the young and addressed them on the great salvation. These loving labours have been so accompanied with the power of the Holy Spirit, that I have no doubt in the great day tens of thousands of children will rise up and call him blessed.

The book already referred to, 'Jesus the Way,' is a description of the Holy Land, and is full of Jesus—unlike the 'Sketches of Palestine' in this respect, that it is specially intended for children, and is eminently calculated to interest them, and draw them lovingly to the Good Shepherd.

In these times there is a prevailing impression that a multitude of children brought together at a meeting cannot be interested except by such expedients as penny readings, magic lanterns, &c. The labours of Mr. Hammond go to show that those who think so do not understand children—their real wants and feelings, and their susceptibilities of deep and abiding religious impressions. Wherever the trial has been fairly made, it has been clearly shown that children—even *little* children—can be led to realize the love of God in Christ Jesus, and that the story of redeeming love has special charms for the young heart. Apart altogether from immediate fruit of a spiritual character attending his labours, Mr. Hammond has in this matter taught all the Churches and all ministers of the Gospel a lesson most precious.

ROBERT KNOX.

BELFAST, *February* 8, 1868.

CONTENTS.

CHAPTER I.

Western Journey—The Mother's Grave—Lines 'To our Mother in Heaven'—The Response . . 1

CHAPTER II.

Crossing the Ocean—The Soul's Longitude—Crystal Palace Fountains—Hampton Court—Visit to Paris 7

CHAPTER III.

View from Rigi—Waterfalls—'All my Springs are in Thee' 12

CHAPTER IV.

Avoiding Quarantine—To Alexandria—Veiled Women—Leaving Egypt 17

CHAPTER V.

Quarantine—Damascus—'The Street called Straight'—View from Kaukab—Naaman's House—Abdel-Kader—Mount Hermon—Lines . . 22

CHAPTER VI.

Commencing the Journey—Sidon—Alexander the Great 31

CHAPTER VII.

Ruins of Sidon—Ras-el-Ain—To Cesarea Philippi—Christ Transfigured—The Gospel—An Entreaty—Consecration—'Looking only to Jesus' 35

CHAPTER VIII.

Sea of Galilee—Leaving Safed—Along the Sea of Tiberias—Galilee by Moonlight—Storm—'A great Storm of Wind'—Prayer answered . 45

CHAPTER IX.

Capernaum—Jairus' Daughter—Lines—'Follow Me' 53

CHAPTER X.

Farewell to Galilee 58

CHAPTER XI.

Christ at Nazareth—Noted Places—Nazareth—Lines 61

CHAPTER XII.

Mount Tabor—Leaving Nazareth—Shunem—Gideon's Victory—'Be not Fearful'. . . 66

CHAPTER XIII.

Jezebel—Dothan—Elisha's Prayer answered—Samaria—Four Lepers—Christ our All—Morning's Dawn—Departed Glory of Samaria . 72

CHAPTER XIV.

Christ at Jacob's Well—The Living Water—The Harvest Fields—Ascent of Gerizim—Christ our Sacrifice—Shiloh—Little Samuel—Jacob's Ladder—Bethel to Jerusalem—Gibeon and Gibeah 81

CHAPTER XV.

Entering Jerusalem—Calvary—Lines Suggested—'Out of every Nation'—'The place where He was Crucified'—Mount of Olives—View from Olivet—Jesus at Bethany—Raising of Lazarus—Christ weeping over Jerusalem—Lines . . 92

CHAPTER XVI.

Mosque of Omar—Altar of Burnt Offering—Mosque-el-Aksa—The Golden Gate—Bethesda—Via Dolorosa—Pilate's Hall—Lines . . . 104

CHAPTER XVII.

Bethany—Cherith and Jericho—Elisha's Fountain—Zaccheus—Blind Bartimeus—Bathing in the Jordan—The Dead Sea—Lines on the Jordan—Sodom—Mar Sabâ—Rebuke to the Monks—Bethlehem—Rachel's Tomb—Solomon's Pools—Hebron—Oak of Mamre—Jerusalem—Pool of Siloam 112

CHAPTER XVIII.

Gethsemane 140

CHAPTER XIX.

Caverns under Jerusalem—Children's Meetings—Crown of Thorns—Ramleh—Russian Princess—Pursuit of a Gazelle—House of Simon the Tanner—Dorcas—Farewell to the Holy Land—To Cairo—Lines on the Ascent of the Pyramids 143

CHAPTER XX.

Mount Etna—Stromboli—Scylla and Charybdis—Naples—Herculaneum and Pompeii—Ascent of Mount Vesuvius—Tomb of Virgil—Baiæ—Children's Meetings—Capua 161

CHAPTER XXI.

Rome—St. Peter's—Mamertine Prison—Catacombs—Pio Nono—Palace of the Cæsars—Florence—Children's Meetings—Mont Cenis—Paris—Glasgow—Oxford—London—Meetings—Rev. Baptist Noel—Conclusion—Lines . . . 171

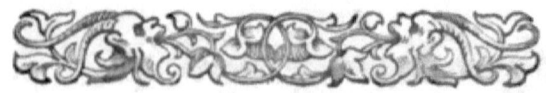

DO I hear you ask, my reader,
Why it was these lines were written?
They were written to give pleasure
To the friends of Edward Payson,
Who might feel inclined to follow
In his footsteps to that country,
Where the Bible first was written,
Where its scenes were all enacted,
Where our Saviour lived and suffered,
Where He gave His life a ransom,
That He might redeem the guilty.

   They were written *con amore*,
Some by sparkling Pharpar's waters,
Near the city of Damascus,
Day by day through Palestina,
Sometimes underneath Mount Hermon;
And, again, by Jordan's waters,
Yea, and in that very garden
Where our blessed Saviour suffered,
Where He sweat those drops of crimson.

   In such places, oh! how hallowed!
Day by day new lines were added.
Some were jotted down in Cairo,
Others on the sands of Egypt,
By the Pyramids so lofty;
Some upon the mighty waters
Of the Nile, the king of rivers;
Others on the Mediterranean,
Following in the apostle's footsteps—
The apostle of the Gentiles.
But as they were not intended

To be read by distant strangers,
With reluctance has the writer
Yielded to his friends' entreaties,
And consented to make public
Words which hastily were written
For kind friends who are indulgent,
And would pardon imperfections.

 Often has the prayer been offered,
That the Lord would add His blessing,
And would make these words a comfort
To the followers of Jesus;
That they might be stimulated
Each to work for God more boldly,
Making it their one endeavour
To lead lost ones to the Saviour.

 Often has the prayer ascended,
That the young might find instruction
In these lines of simple measure,
That they each might hear of Jesus,
Of His wondrous incarnation,
Of His life so pure and holy,
Of His death so full of anguish,
That they might obtain forgiveness.

 In these pages is the Gospel,
The glad tidings of salvation
Through a dead and risen Saviour.

 If they only cause the reader
God's Word earnestly to study,
And to find its hidden treasures;
If they help to make more vivid
Bible scenes herein depicted;
If they lead to holy living,
To a firmer trust in Jesus;
If they point to Christ the Saviour,
Some one seeking peace and pardon,—
Then their object is accomplished,
And the writer well rewarded.

SKETCHES OF PALESTINE.

CHAPTER I.

IN the month[1] that is so lovely,
When all Nature's clothed in verdure,
On a bright and sunny May-day—
Then it was a happy couple,
Hopeful, stood by Hymen's altar.
It was then that they both plighted,
In the presence of their Master,
That they would forsake all others,
And in love cling to each other,
In the storm and in the sunshine,
In the days of grief and sadness,
As well as in days of gladness.

Thus it was they were united,
By the man of God appointed
To perform the solemn union.

Then, whene'er the word was spoken,
And the fervent prayer was offered,
After greetings from their parents,
* * * *
And the many friends assembled,
Round the festive board they gathered.
Loaded with the richest viands,

[1] May 24, 1866.

Where all talked and laughed together,
And each eye was bright with gladness.
   Then they hastened to Niagara.
        *   *   *   *

There they heard their Master calling,
'Go and work within my vineyard,
And my presence shall go with thee.'
Quickly they obeyed the summons.
On the lovely banks of Erie,
With the godly Mr. Howland,
There they gathered in the harvest,
Working with the Holy Spirit,
Winning souls to Christ their Master.
        *   *   *   *   *

   Down to Springfield then they journeyed,
Soon the children thronged to meet them
In great numbers in the capital;
Also, 'neath the dome of Heaven
Fifty hundred people gathered,
All to listen to the message,
Coming from Jehovah's servant.
   After standing by the tomb-stone
Of the noble Abram Lincoln,
Then they turned their steps to Rockford,
Where the Sabbath-school convention
Met for mutual instruction
In the truths of Zion's welfare.
There they saw large crowds of children
Flocking quickly to the Saviour.
God was with them in their journey,
Thus their words were blessed to many.
   Then away to great Chicago,
And across the plains of Canada
To the broad and beauteous Hudson,
They came to the lovely valley
Of the 'land of steady habits.'

THE MOTHER'S GRAVE.

There they dwelt for weeks together
In the place where Edward Payson
Had been taught by his dear mother
In the ways of heavenly wisdom.
  O'er the hills they often wandered
Where he had in days of boyhood
Sported with his youthful playmates;
There they saw his dear old father,
Who had lived years six and seventy;
Heard his words in prayer ascending
For a blessing on his children.
  To the quiet village grave-yard,
To the place where his dear mother
Sleeps the sleep that knows no waking
Till the resurrection morning,
There they knelt and prayed together,
That the prayers their mother offered
In the days when, like a sunbeam,
All were gladdened in her presence,
Might descend in richest blessings,
As they o'er life's pathway journeyed.
Ere they left that spot so hallowed,
They renewed their consecration
To their risen Lord and Master,
Knowing that if they were faithful,
They should one day meet their mother
In the land of the Hereafter.
  While they stood beside that tomb-stone,
With their fond and loving sisters,
And their nieces and their nephews,
E. repeated there these stanzas
He'd addressed his sainted mother[1]
Just as she was borne by angels
To the presence of her Saviour,

[1] February 7, 1865.

There to meet departed loved ones
And to wait for others coming:

Dearest mother, thou hast left us!
   Left us for a happier clime,
God our Father hath bereft us,
   We shall meet no more in time;
But we soon shall meet in heaven,
   Where all tears are wiped away;
Meet to part no more for ever,
   Through fruition's perfect day.

All thy sorrows now are ended,
   Thou again shalt never sigh;
Now in praise thy voice is blended
   With angelic choirs on high.
Oft our eyes are dim with weeping,
   But we will not weep for thee,
For we know that thou art reaping
   Joys through all eternity.

'Dearest Jesus, oh, come quickly:'
   Was thy plaintive, longing cry;
When He came to bear thee heavenward,
   Oh, what joy lit up thine eye!
Volumes, volumes, thou didst speak then
   With those bright expressive eyes
Ere the Saviour gently closed them,
   Bearing thee to yonder skies.

O that we may never falter
   In the path which thou hast trod!
Oft we'll meet around the altar
   Where thy prayers went up to God.
When at last we too are summoned,
   Each to lay our armour down,
May we then with thee be numbered,
   And receive the promised crown.

MOTHER'S RESPONSE TO HER LOVED ONES.

Mourn not that I've closed my mission;
   Loved ones, now rejoice with me;
Hope I've changed to glad fruition,
   Now my soul from sin is free.
Blessed Jesus, He received me,
   Opening wide His loving arms;
All through life He ne'er deceived me,
   Death to me had no alarms.

When the precious Saviour took me
   In His gentle arms above,
All my sorrows then forsook me;
   Now I dwell where all is love.
Yes, my soul is full of gladness,
   Jesus is my 'all in all;'
Here is nought of sin nor sadness,
   Heaven's pleasures never pall.

Jesus leads me to the 'river,'
    Where the 'crystal' waters flow ;
I shall thirst again, no, never !
    And fatigue I ne'er shall know.
Heaven dreads no death nor sorrow,
    Nought of sickness nor of pain ;
Anxious fears about the morrow
    I shall never feel again.

'Clouds of witnesses' encompass
    Those who run the heavenly race ;
O then, 'looking unto Jesus,'
    Daily trust in Him for grace.
He will make you 'wise' in winning
    Weary wanderers to his fold ;
He will keep you each from sinning,
    Bring you to the final goal.

    Finally, the day was dawning
When they from these scenes must sever,
And must hasten on their journey
To the Holy Land of Promise.

    *   *   *   *

CHAPTER IL

NUMEROUS were the friends that gathered,
When in the good ship 'Hibernia,'
They weighed anchor in the harbour
Of the Metropolitan City.
It would take too long to narrate
All the many things that happened
In their voyage across the ocean.
God was with them, and preserved them
From the dangers they encountered
On the wild and stormy billows.
As they journeyed ever eastward,
They observed their watches losing
Day by day some twenty minutes.
With this fact was taught a lesson
E. embodied in these verses:

  As o'er the deep blue sea we sail,
   With ever-hastening speed,
  If we the rising sun would hail,
   The *true* time we must heed.

  Our watches we do always find
   Are losing time each day;
  And if we would not be behind,
   We must not heed their say.

If we would keep them with the sun,
    They must be daily set;
For soon they far behind would run
    If we should this forget.

Thus as we sail o'er life's rough sea,
    Most surely we shall find
That as we nearer draw to Christ,
    The world is left behind.

And should they chance to think it strange
    We cease 'with them to run,'
Then we can tell them we have changed
    As we approach the sun.

Yes, we can tell them we have not
    That longitude of soul,
Which we once had when we set out
    To reach the heavenly goal.

As toward the Sun of Righteousness
    We evermore draw nigh,
Like His will be our glorious dress
    When we are called to die.

Then landed safe beyond life's sea,
    We ne'er from Christ shall part,
But in all perfect harmony
    We shall be one in heart.

CRYSTAL PALACE FOUNTAINS.

 O how happy ! O how joyous
Were their hearts to see old Scotland !
Many were the friends who hailed them,
Thinking of the time when Edward
Preached to them the glorious Gospel,
With the Spirit's demonstration.
 Many days flew by them quickly,
Spent among the lakes and mountains
Of the wild romantic Highlands,
Which Sir Walter has made classic.
 Ne'er will they forget the kindness
Shown them by a Glasgow merchant,
At his residence in Greenock,
Where, upon the water's borders,
He looks out upon a landscape
Full of rich, majestic beauty,
Where the mountains, in the background—
The old 'Cobbler' and Ben Lomond—
Towering high reveal their glory.
 Thence away they sped to London—
That great city of three million.
Many were the scenes they witnessed,
Full of deep and wondrous interest.
 With full forty thousand people
Were they at the Crystal Palace,
To behold the marvellous fire-works
And th' illuminated fountains,
Which, with lights all different tinted,
Looked like liquid fires volcanic.
 Those same fountains oft are playing,
But they ne'er attract the people
As when thus illuminated.
Thus it was they were reminded,
That the waters of salvation
Should be made to all attractive
With the clearest illustrations,

Lighted up with pleasing story,—
Parables such as the Saviour
Often used when He was preaching;
For 'tis said that He without them
Never spake unto the people.

   Well they knew the Holy Spirit
Only blesses *truth* that's covered
With the words that may be uttered.
Yet they knew that when upon it
Light was made to be reflected
From the objects to all common,
It was sought for by the people,
Who might otherwise have passed it
Without any thought or feeling.

   Hampton Court, twelve miles from London,
With its deer-parks and its gardens,
With its lovely sparkling fountains,
With its labyrinths so winding,
Where King Henry often wandered,
Much it claimed of their attention.
There within the picture galleries,
Long they gazed upon the paintings
Of the celebrated masters.

   Oft they thought of Cardinal Wolsey;
He, the builder of the palace,
How he rose to be the ruler
Of the king and of the country;
How at last his sins o'ertook him,
Robbing him of all his honour,
Leading him in bitter anguish
To exclaim, 'Had I as faithful
Been to God as to King Henry,
He would not have given me over
When my hair with grey was silvered.'

   London Tower, of course, they visited;
Saw the room where Walter Raleigh

For twelve years was once imprisoned;
Yet not idle, for he wrote there
Of the world, its varied history.
   In the cell they also entered
Where the wife of wicked Henry,
She, the lovely, beauteous Anna,
Was shut up until beheaded.
   After spending weeks in London,
Then they crossed the English Channel
To the gay and lovely Paris.
Full of beauty and of fashion,
There they saw what some call freedom.
But, alas! it was *false* freedom,
Freedom to commit much evil,
Freedom full to break the Sabbath,
Freedom to plunge into vices
Ruinous to souls and bodies
Of, alas! too many thousands.
Of *true* freedom they saw little.
   In the lovely Champs Elysées
Theatres upon the Sabbath
To profane its sacred hours.
These were granted perfect freedom,
Yea, protection from the *gens d'armes*.
But if on the ground a preacher
Of the pure and simple Gospel
Should rise up to speak of Jesus,
Of his precious love in dying
In our stead, that He might purchase
For us full and free salvation,
He would quickly there be silenced,
Or, perchance be led to prison.
   God in mercy grant that Paris
May be free from all such freedom!
May the blessed time be hastened
When the Lord shall make them freemen—
Free from Satan's snares and slavery.

CHAPTER III.

THEN to Switzerland they hasted;
　　Stopped at Zurich, where lived Zwingle,
　　He, the great and bold Reformer,
Who laid down his life the rather
Than to see religion suffer.
　There they saw the house he dwelt in,
Now within it are sold Bibles,
Saw the grand cathedral, in which
He proclaimed the precious Gospel
To the people of his Canton,
When the glorious Reformation
Just was dawning on the nations.
　Still within that same cathedral
Christ is preached in all His fulness;
Yes, the peasants of that Canton
Still are reaping the rich harvest
From the seed there sown by Zwingle.
O how true, that good men's labours
'Follow them' throughout the centuries!
　Lovely, charming, was Lake Zurich
On that bright September morning,
When, with Doctor B., from Brooklyn,
And his wife, the happy couple
Sailed for Rigi, that high mountain
Which all tourists always visit,
That they may behold the sun rise
O'er the lofty Alpine mountains,

Tinging first the virgin snow-peaks,
Where the foot of man has never
Soiled the snow so pure and spotless.
   First, when all was black and dreary,
When the lower mounts and valleys
Each were shrouded in thick darkness,
Towering high in air above them,
Sparkling like some mighty diamond,
Rose the Wetter Horn majestic,
Catching the first light of morning,
When all else was veiled and hidden.
Soon another rose up blushing,
Changing colour every moment
In the glance of bright Aurora.
   Finally the lower mountains
One by one revealed their features,
As the sun, in all his glory,
Flooded them with golden sunlight,
Till at length the veil of darkness
Quite was lifted from the landscape,
Showing them where had been sleeping
'Leven lakes of matchless beauty,
Near which many towns and cities
Added to the charming prospect.
   From Lucerne they passed o'er Brunig,
To the wondrous falls of Geesbach,
Where, with fourteen leaps, the water
Thunders down into the valley.
These at night they then saw lighted
Up with Bengal lights, all glowing
With the beauties of the rainbow.
Hundreds gathered in the darkness
To behold that sight so wondrous.
   Thus, when truth is made attractive,
Sinners flock to see its beauty.
   Interlacken, Lauterbrunen,

Splugen, Berne, and marvellous Regats,
Grindenwald, and many places,
Famous for their wondrous scenery,
Much delighted the four pilgrims,
Who had turned aside a little
From their way to Palestina.
   Oft their notice was attracted
By the houses, perched, like birds' nests,
On the crags of lofty mountains.
How the people lived so high up
Was to them a serious problem—
Not a foot of ground was wasted.
   Thus they prayed that God would help them,
Be as diligent in tilling
Their own hearts, that they might flourish
With the healthful fruits of piety.
   They were also much astonished,
As they gazed upon the fountains,
Gushing from the tops of mountains.
How did floods of water get there?
For it seemed that in an hour
All the waters would be emptied
From those barren-looking headlands.
   But they flow the same as ever,
Never failing in their treasure.
   Then they thought of living Christians,
All whose 'springs' are in the Saviour,
And who, while they 'water others,'
Are themselves thus always watered;
And of Jesu's precious promise,
'He that drinketh of the water
That by Me is freely given,
He shall thirst again, no, never.'
Then it was that Edward Payson
Wrote these simple lines of poetry,
Setting forth this truth important:—

'ALL MY SPRINGS ARE IN THEE.'

Travellers 'mid the Alpine glade,
   Oft are gladdened with the sight
Of the joyous, bright cascade
   Leaping from a wondrous height.
To beholders it appears,
   That within but one brief hour,
All their waters, dried like tears,
   Soon would cease the vale to shower.

Oft it seems a mystery,
   Whence these waters ever flow,
Still they bound as light and free,
   Never caring we should know;
High up almost in the sky
   Are their rich but hidden springs,
Whence they to the valleys fly,
   While all nature round them sings.

Thus the Christian, much with God,
   Watered with the heavenly dew,
Brings from the divine abode
   Blessings that are fresh and new.
He can ever truly say,
   '*All my springs, Lord, are in Thee;*
Watering others every day,
   Still, my Father, water me.'

If by Christ we're daily taught,
   We shall often hear His voice—

'Without me ye can do nought,
   Drink Life's water, and rejoice,
For 'tis true that whosoever
   Drinks of water that I give,
He shall thirst again, no, never—
   Like a fountain he shall live.'

CHAPTER IV.

MANY weeks they spent in seeking
For some way to get to Syria,
Without being shut in prison
In some hideous Lazaretto.
  Having crossed the Alps by Splugen,
Several days they spent in Milan.
  Oft they visited its cathedral,
From its top the panorama
On all sides was most enchanting,
Like a wall of purest marble
Rose the Alps in lofty grandeur—
Crowning all was Monte Rosa,
With its shining robe of crimson
Sparkling in the light of heaven.
  In Milan they saw the painting
Of our Lord with His disciples,
On the eve of crucifixion—
Master-work of Leonardo,
Who for sixteen years was busied
In the work ere 'twas completed.
  After seeing Milan's wonders,
Then away they sped to Venice,
Where there are no streets nor horses,
Where no carriage ever rumbles,
Where instead the gondolier
Plies his oar to sweetest music
Wafted on the air so balmy—

'Tis the place to give to painters,
And to poets, inspiration.
   On the Bridge of Sighs they lingered
O'er which pris'ners oft were taken
From the palace to the dungeon,
Or perchance to execution.
   Halcyon days were those in Venice,
Revelling among its paintings,
And its works of art so numerous.
   Thence across the Adriatic
To Trieste, an Austrian city,
And thro' it to great Vienna,
Where once lived Maria Theresa,
And the kings and queens of Austria,
And where still their hearts are resting.
   Tho' the Austrians were humbled
By the recent Prussian vict'ries,
Still their city was attractive,
Shonbrunn Palace and its fountains
And its gardens, oh! how lovely.
   One bright morning, on the Danube
They embarked for Constantinople;
Of the Rhine they oft were thinking
As they swiftly passed the castles.
   In the capital of Hungary,
They received a sad, sad message,
O'er the wires from Constantinople
Came the Sultan's message to them,
'All who enter this our city
First must stay in Lazaretto,—
If they from it should make trial
To escape, they would most surely
Carefully be shot *instanter*
And most *carelessly* be buried.'
   Therefore then their course they altered,
Their first station was to Salzburg,

At the same hotel was Motley,
Author of the *Dutch Republic,*
Thence to Inspruck o'er the Brenner
Pass to Italy they hastened,
Eighty miles the distance travelled
O'er the mountain drawn by horses.

While they tarried at Verona,
There they saw the Amphitheatre,
Holding over twenty thousands,
Where once fought the gladiators.

On and on thro' many cities,
Thro' Bologna to Ancona,
Stopping oft to see the places
Mentioned in the classic history.

Down the eastern coast of Italy,
By a route not much frequented,
Therefore far more interesting,—
Finally they reached Brendissi,
Where they found a steamer waiting
To convey them o'er to Egypt,
To the city Alexandria.

On their left the Isles of Greece were
Beautiful and full of interest.

Three days of delightful sailing
Brought them safe to Africa's harbour,
To the City of Apollos,
He the 'eloquent and mighty,'
'Mighty in the Holy Scriptures,'
To the city where St. Marcus
Preached the Gospel to the people
Till they rose in fury on him,
Dragging him from street to street till
All his breath had left his body,
And his spirit had ascended
Where the wicked cease from troubling.

But when fairly in that harbour

All their thoughts were of the present,
Mark, Apollos, St. Augustine
Were not thought of in the hubbub,
But the motley crowd around them
Of all costumes and all nations,—
Arabs, speaking broken English,
Nubians, black as blackest ebony,
English, French, and turbaned Moslems,
These absorb their whole attention.

Through the midst of this excitement,
Crowds of boys and braying donkeys,
Walked the camels, calm and stately,
They the slow ships of the desert.

There it was they first saw women
Veiled from head to foot in muslin,
In accordance with the custom
Of the Moslems, so degraded;
Oh! how much in Christian countries,
Does each woman owe the Saviour;
She to Him owes her position
As an equal and a partner
With the sex some call the 'sterner.'

Where the knowledge of His sufferings,
And His death for guilty sinners,
Is not known—'tis there that woman
Is ill-treated all her life-time.

Such, O woman! had your fate been
Had you not lived in the country
Where the Gospel scheme is published.

Do you love that precious Saviour,
To whom you are such a debtor,
'Thro' whose death you reap enjoyment,
Rich indeed, yet oft forgotten?
Sure, if not, your heart is hardened,
God's own goodness has not led you
To repentance and obedience,

LEAVING EGYPT.

    Pray at once to Him for pardon,
Asking for the sake of Jesus
To forgive you for not loving
Him from whom come all our blessings.
    After seeing Pompey's pillar,
Cleopatra's needle also,
And the sights of Lower Egypt,
For Beyrout they then took steamer,
Anxious, eager, oh! how eager,
To set foot on Palestina,
And to see that holy city
Where our blessed Lord was wounded,
For a ruined world's salvation.

CHAPTER V.

AFTER several days of sailing
On the classic Mediterranean,
One bright morning they dropped anchor
In the harbour of Berytus.
Numerous were the invitations
From old friends within the city
To accept their hospitality,
But imperious was the summons
Of an officer of the 'sick man,'
Quick to hasten to the quarters
Of the suburb *Quarantinus*.
Well they knew what was the motive
Which induced him to delay them
On their way to Palestina.
All his coffers were impoverished
By his debts, which were too numerous
For his weak and slender income.
They were therefore each imprisoned
Eight long days in narrow quarters,
Altho' not one on their ship-board
Had with cholera been tainted.
But tho' with high walls surrounded,
Still their thoughts afar could wander;—
So to friends across the water
Oft they sent some cheering message.
Books in numbers were not wanting,
And with friends with voices cheerful,

Hour by hour flew past so quickly
That their stay in Quarantina
After all was not so tedious
As they had anticipated.
    Oft to them it was annoying
Just to watch their guardianos,
While they followed them as closely
As if they were hourly seeking
To escape unto the mountains.
    Oft they thought of Paul at Roma,
Ever chained fast to a soldier.
Tho' their friends, the missionaries,
Often came with words to cheer them,
Still their guardianos watched them
Lest they should shake hands together,
For they knew if once they touched them
They would surely be imprisoned
Ten long days in Quarantina.
    When their time was full accomplished,
Quick they drove to Beyrout City
And received the kindest welcome
From the dear-loved missionaries.
    Soon the children all were gathered,
Greeks and Moslems, Jews and Maronites,
With the Druses from Mount Lebanon,
Side by side they sat together,
While they told them of their Saviour,
Who had died for them on Calvary.
    Oh! how pleasant 'twas to see them
By God's Spirit much affected,
All because they were so sinful
In not loving the dear Saviour,
Who had for their sins been wounded
On the brow of Calvary's mountain.
    Some, we trust, of those dear children
Learned to love the dear Redeemer.

Finally, one day they started
In the diligence for Damascus,
That most ancient of all cities,
Which existed even when Abram
Lived with his beloved Sarah,
Tenting in the Land of Promise,
When not hastening to Damascus
In pursuit of Chedorlaomer.
   Up Mount Lebanon so lofty
Quick they flew with fleetest horses.
   Feet, five thousand and six hundred
Was the height they soon attained to.
   To the left they saw Mount Sunin,
Rising feet full twice five thousand,
Clad in robes of snowy whiteness,
Just as in the days the Prophets
And the Apostles gazed upon it.
Crossing also Anti-Lebanon—
Twelve miles distant from the other,
Then upon them burst the valley
Through which runs the river Pharpar
And the Abana so sparkling,
On whose banks were beauteous gardens,
Loaded with rich fruit delicious.
   O how strange were their emotions,
As they drove into that city
Where Naaman lived, the Leper,
And where cruel King Ben-hadad
Ruled his people Oriental!
   Where, too, Paul, with blindness smitten,
Once was led in utter darkness
To the house of one called Judas,[1]
There to wait till Ananias
Came with words of cheering comfort,
As he was by God appointed.

[1] Acts ix. 11.

But to them it seemed more wondrous
When they visited the places
Which within God's word are mentioned,
Sure they were that they then traversed
O'er the street that Paul had walked in,
That their eyes gazed on the pillars,
Beautiful Corinthian columns,
Which had borne up the high arches,
Under which the Apostle lingered
When disputing with the people,
Who had heard him in the temple,
Oft declaring that the Naz'rene
Was none other than Messiah.

O how cruel 'twas to hate him,
All because he kindly told them
Of the finished work of Jesus,
When He suffered on the mountain!

'Twas no wonder that the pilgrims
Searched with interest for the window
From which he escaped with safety,
That his life might not be taken.

Pleasant was it also for them
To be pointed to the tombstone
Of Saint George the Christian martyr,
Who assisted the Apostle
From the window o'er the portal,
All because he loved the Saviour,
And was willing, like a martyr,
To be torn in pieces rather
Than to see so true a soldier
Sacrificed to brutal violence.

Pleasant was it for the travellers
Oft to fix their eyes on Kaukab,
On that little ruined village
Where 'tis said Paul met the Saviour,
Who in words that pierced his soul through,

Asked him why he dared to persecute
Him, the risen Lord of Glory.
  Oh, what thoughts then pressed upon them,
As they gazed upon that landscape
Paul himself looked on, while threatenings
From his lips against the Christians
Forth were sent with fiercest utterance.
  On his left then stood Mount Hermon,
Towering high in feet ten thousand,
Robed in snow of shining whiteness.
  But about him was a brightness
Which exceeded the reflection
Of the noon-day sun on Hermon.
On his right flowed past the Pharpar,
On his left the clear Abana,
And before him lay the city
'Neath the noon-day sun all quiet,
Robed in richest emerald beauty.
  But when Christ the Saviour met him,
All his thoughts turned from the scenery
Of the fair enchanting landscape.
All his sins came quick before him,
Then he saw that while he hated
Those who loved the name of Jesus,
While he sought to persecute them,
And to cast them into prison,
He was also persecuting
At the same time the Messiah.
'Tis no wonder when he felt this
That he there was filled with trembling,
And that he was so astonished,
That his strength then quickly left him,
Filled with sorrow and submission.
  Thus the past came up before them
As they looked on ancient Kaukab.
Pleasant was the hour the party

Spent in seeing where Naaman,[1]
Captain of the hosts of Syria,
He the mighty man of valour
Lived in luxury and splendour,
Yet unhappy all because that
He was still a wretched leper.
True they saw there nought but ruins,
Yet they, in imagination,
Saw the little maid of Israel
Speaking to the wife of Naaman
Of the prophet in Samaria,
Who could quickly cure her master.
    From a massive fallen column
They broke off a little fragment ;
From a fig-tree near the hearthstone,
Gathered also they a fig-leaf,
That they might in lands far distant,
Better call to mind the ruins
Of the house of the great captain
Of the mighty hosts of Syria.
    While among the ruins wandering,
O how sad were they to find there
That the place where once lived Naaman
Now was a drear Lazaretto.
    O how sad and how astonished
Were they to behold nine lepers,
Men and women, real lepers,
Dying daily and yet living
Always with the fear of dying.
    What a picture were the lepers,
Of our race, with sin all poisoned,
Each one needing the Physician
Who alone from death can save them.
Blessings to Him, He has opened
Up a fountain that will cleanse all

[1] 2 Kings v. 1.

Who will wash in its clear waters.
For 'tis written in God's volume
That the blood of His Son Jesus
Cleanseth from all sins' pollutions.
   Ere they left the ancient city
Their steps turned to the good consul
Of the great American people.
   Though an Arab, yet a Christian,
Yea, a most devoted champion
Of the rich and glorious Gospel.
   Then with tearful eyes he told them
How that Doctor King, of Athens,
Kindly led him to the Saviour.
A great scar upon his forehead,
They there saw which in the massacre
Was inflicted by the Moslems,
When they slew within the city,
Full two thousand and five hundred.
   Then they went to Abdel-Kader,
He, the much renowned Algerian
Who defended many Christians
In the time of that vile slaughter,
When through all the plains of Syria,
Far away down to Hasbeiya,
Full six thousand there were murdered.
   They can ne'er forget the beauty
Of his brow, so broad, majestic,
And his pleasant face so radiant.
When they spoke of his great kindness
In defending in the castle,
With his soldiers from Algeria,
Those who bore the name of Christians,
Simple was his answer to them,
'I but only did my duty,
And to God be all the glory.'
   Finally from old Damascus

To Beyrout they turned their faces.
Very early in the morning
They took leave of kind Demetrius,
And just as the sun was rising,
While they were Mount Lebanon climbing,
On their view then burst Mount Hermon
Full of majesty and glory.
  Quick the heart of Edward Payson
Was inspired to write some verses.
Well he knew he was no poet,
Still to him it was a pleasure
To jot down these lines, tho' simple,
Which so quickly pressed upon him.
I shall venture to transcribe them
Word for word as they were written
In the carriage o'er the mountain :—

  Mine eyes on Hermon rested,
    Just at the break of day,
  Its brow with snow was crested,
    Where the bright sunbeams lay.
  What thoughts then pressed upon me
    As on that mount I gazed,
  I lived not in the present,
    But in long by-gone days.

  I thought of how the Saviour
    Had looked upon those flights,
  And how he had ascended
    To one of its great heights.
  Of His transfiguration,
    In which His lovely face

Shone with a heavenly brightness,
    No pencil e'er can trace.

That scene I once saw painted
    By Raphael's wondrous power,
And oft within Rome's Vatican
    Gazed on it by the hour.
But when I looked on **Hermon**,
    Imagination then
Portrayed the scene with more of life
    Than e'er did Raphael's pen.

It seemed to me no wonder
    That **Peter** would remain
With Jesus on the mountain,
    And ne'er remove again.
If e'er before he'd doubted
    That Jesus was divine,
His doubts then quickly vanished
    In that bright halo's shine.

'Twas from that cloud he heard then
    The voice of God declare,
'This is my Son beloved,
    Let him thy full trust share.'
Thanks be to God the Father,
    We live in this bright day,
When but the Spirit's needed,
    To point to Christ the way.

CHAPTER VI.

'TWAS the fourteenth of November,
Bright and glorious was the morning,
When they started from the city
Which of yore was called Berytus,
Where the dear-loved missionaries
Entertained them all so kindly.
Only four were in their party—
One, a Doctor B. from Brooklyn,
Learnèd in the Holy Scriptures,
Much beloved by his people;
With his wife, who, like a sunbeam,
Made those happy all around her.

Each on horses were well mounted,
One from Persia o'er the desert,
Others Syrian in their lineage.
All were full of life and spirit,
Eager, restless, for the journey.

For their leader they had Michael,
Better known as Michael Haney.
He, of all the men of Syria,
Was the truest and the boldest.
O'er his shoulder hung a musket—
In his belt a good revolver,
To drive off the Bedouin robbers,
Who infest the mountain passes.
Arabic was his native language,
Yet he knew well how to talk with

Men from far across the water.
He could speak with men from Italy,
With the French, and with the Germans,
With the Turks, and with the English,
Also men from classic Athens,
He could talk with in their language.
So they learned to trust him fully,
Nothing cared they for the Bedouins.
 Closely followed with the good things,
Mustapha, the Moslem Hadji,
Having long since been to Mecca.
Eighteen were the mules and horses
Which were needed to convey them,
With their tents, and with their luggage,
O'er the hills, and through the valleys
Of the Holy Land of Promise.
 The first day they rode eight hours,
Passing close along the sea-shore,
Where 'tis said the Prophet Jonah,
Once escaped from the embraces,
Of that huge aquatic monster
Which three days had tightly held him.
 Just at sunset they reached Sidon,
Once, indeed, a prosperous city,
Erst the curse of God was on it,
For the sins which it committed.
 There they saw the holy prophets
Spake most truly when they uttered
Against Sidon maledictions.
 Oh, how graphic seemed Ezekiel,
As they read his words in Sidon!
All her palaces are fallen—
Only a few scattered columns
Could be found there to remind them
Of the wealth of the 'Great Sidon.'
 Then they called to mind its capture,

By the Persian Shalmaneser,
B.C. seven hundred twenty,
And how, when it once revolted
From the mighty rule of Persia,
Artaxerxes came and took it,
Killing many of her people.

And they thought of Alexander,
He, who o'er the world once triumphed,
And then wept, because another
Was not found for him to conquer,
Came and summoned its surrender,
And how it, without a struggle,
Opened quick its gates unto him.

O how true 'tis that transgressors
Find the ways of sin oppressive
To themselves and to their children!
Where was once proud Sidon's city,
Full of wealth and full of beauty,
With its teeming population,
And its harbour full of shipping,
Now, alas! are wretched hovels,
Built of mud and ancient ruins.

Very cheering was it for them
There to find two missionaries
Preaching to the wretched people
Of the finished work of Jesus,
Seeking thus to elevate them
From the depths of degradation.

As they passed from out the city,
Soon they came to excavations
Going on among the ashes,
Deep down in the rocky caverns
Of the ancient kings of Sidon,
Where were found coins, gold and silver,
Some stamped with the royal impress
Of King Philip, King of Macedon,

And his son, Great Alexander.
Not a single trace remaineth
On those massive stones of marble,
To make known to passing travellers,
Who, three thousand years now by-gone,
There were once laid down in silence—
All were kings, and yet forgotten.

   Thus, from far across the water,
Strangers come and search for treasures,
Or some curious antique relics,
Shedding light upon past ages.

CHAPTER VII.

HAVING bid adieu to Sidon,
　　Ere the sun had reached its zenith,
　　On they journeyed to Sarepta.[1]
Now, alas! 'tis all in ruins,
Scarce one stone upon another
Of the ancient town remaineth
To point out where once the widow
Met Elijah, the good prophet,
Who sustained her in the famine,
While around were many dying.
　On that spot perchance 'twas also
That the Saviour met the woman,
Who in great distress was crying,
'Jesus, oh! have mercy on me,
For my daughter she is dying,
Vexèd with an evil spirit!'
　When he saw her importunity,
Coupled with her deep humility,
Quick His heart was moved with pity,
And He said, 'O woman, let it
Be to thee as thou desirest.'
　'Tis no wonder that the pilgrims
Offered there the prayer most fervent,
'More of faith, O Saviour, teach us,
That we may not lose the blessing
For the want of earnest pleading!'

[1] 1 Kings xvii. 9.

After eight hours in their saddle,
As the glorious sun was sinking
To his couch, all decked with crimson,
Then it was the weary travellers
Rode along by Paletyrus.
Rather o'er its ruins they went,
Seeking for their own encampment.

Soon they found it near the columns,
Cast long since by Alexander,
All along beside the sea-shore.

Tent life to them then was novel.
Soon a rich repast was served them
From the bounteous stores of Michael.

After dinner they read over
All that's in the Holy Bible
About Tyre, the wicked city,
Which for its vile sins was punished,
And destroyed by God from heaven.

O how graphic seemed Ezekiel,[1]
How exact were his descriptions,
Even of the very manner,
Of the city's desolation.

Having in their tents slept soundly,
The next morning they rose early.
Tho' it was November seventeenth,
They were in the ocean bathing,
Swimming round among the columns,
And among the sunken capitols
That upheld the Syrian temple,
Even in the time of David.

Then they went to the cathedral
Where, 'tis said, the good Eusebius,
Who is called one of the Fathers,
Preached the dedication sermon,
In about the year four hundred.

[1] Ezek. vii.

There the bones of Barbarossa,
Far from Salzburg, where his home was,
In great state were once deposited.
　Once it was the fairest temple
That was built in all Phœnicia;
But, alas! its double columns,
All cut out from light, red granite,
And its lofty walls are ruins.
　Then they rode along the sea-shore,
Toward the celebrated fountains,
Where is found the colouring murex,
Treasured up in beauteous sea-shell,
From which came the Syrian purple,
Of which Tyre's daughters boasted.
　Thence to Ras-el-ain they hastened,
Where the sparkling waters issued
From the fountains of King Hiram,
Flowing all the way from Bagdad,
Through an excavated channel. (?)
Now, alas! none drink its waters,
Except a few passing travellers,
Looking on the ancient cities,
Which long since have been destroyed
By the fiat of Jehovah,
For their sins against High Heaven.
　Far away upon a hill-top,
Three miles further on their journey,
They approached the tomb of Hiram,
Friend and ally of King Solomon.
There for now three thousand years
It has stood in solemn grandeur.
　All the other kings of Tyrus
Long since now have been forgotten,
And their tombs to dust have crumbled.
　Over hills and through the valleys,
Up high mountains, on they hastened,

Till they reached the ancient Tibnen,
Under the Crusader's Castle,
Where their tents were waiting for them.
   Their next rest was at Meis-el-Jebl,
In a sheik's house, filled with insects
Far too numerous for their comfort.
   But they helped to start them early
The next morning on their journey.
   On their way to Cesarea
They had many glorious prospects,
From the mountain tops ascended.
Then they saw the Jordan's valley,
And the waters of Lake Merom,
'Side which Joshua smote King Jabin,
Burning all his splendid chariots.
While at Dan they saw the fountain
Forming one of Jordan's sources,
Where at once it bursts a river,
From beneath its rocky strata.
   Now, alas! there's not a dwelling
On the site which marked the boundary
Of the northern coast of Israel.
   Once at Cesarea Philippi,[1]
O how sacred were their feelings!
For they ne'er before were conscious
That their feet had truly trodden
Where once pressed their Saviour's footsteps.
   There they looked upon the mountains
Where our Lord was once transfigured,
In the presence of the prophets,
Who appeared in shining glory,
Speaking to our blessed Saviour
Of the death he should accomplish
For a guilty world's redemption.

[1] Mark viii. 27.

O how sacred seemed Mount Hermon
To the travellers at Banias!
For they knew its rocks had listened,
When a voice from the blue heaven
Sounded clearly in their hearing,
'Hear My Son; He's My Beloved.'
  Somewhere near where they were wandering,
Jesus coming from the mountain,
Doubtless met the anxious father,
Crying, 'On my son have mercy,
Vexèd with an evil spirit;
Thy disciples cannot help him.'
  Quickly then the loving Saviour
From the boy cast out the spirit,
Which had him so oft afflicted.
  How they wished they could have been there
When His followers gathered round him,
Saying, 'Why were we not able
To cast out the evil spirit?'
That we might have heard His answer,
'"Twas because of not believing;
If of faith you had a little,
Even as a grain of mustard,
You might say unto this mountain,
Be thou quickly hence removed,
And your words they would be heeded.
You with faith can always triumph.
True it is this kind, however,
Only goes with prayer and fasting.'
  Much they read within their guide-book,
All about the ancient city;
Of its beauteous marble temple,—
Heathen temple built by Herod,
Dedicated to Augustus.
Long they tarried at the fountain,
Bursting from beneath the rubbish

Of that temple built by Herod.
Near the cave beneath the mountain
Many, many were the ruins
Scattered all along the hill-side;
But how true that all they saw there
Only spake to them of Jesus.

   Of that fountain He had tasted,
'Neath that rock so high and shelving,
He no doubt had often rested.
Through that gate of massive structure,
In the wall around the city,
He had passed with His disciples.

   Perchance it was there that Peter,
Questioned by the Lord of Glory,
Answered, 'Thou art Christ from Heaven,
Son of God, the Mighty Saviour.'

   Bright and cheerful was the morning
When the party entered Kedesh,[1]
Which so long afforded refuge
For the guiltless, who by chance had
Put to death one of their neighbours.

   O how strange were their sensations,
As they rode along the valley,
Where they knew had often hastened,
Covered o'er with perspiration,
Breathless, bleeding at the nostrils,
Many, many who were fleeing
From the blood-avenger's dagger,
Who was seeking to destroy them
Ere they reached the place of refuge,
Knowing that, once in the city,
They could never wreak their vengeance
On the slayers of their kindred.

   Then they could not help but thinking

---

[1] Josh. xx. 7.

Of the guilty sinner fleeing
From the Law, his great avenger,
Armed with vengeance to destroy him,
Fleeing for his own salvation
To the only mighty Refuge
From the wrath of God offended.
　O how like to Christ was Kedesh,
Throwing open wide its portals,
Thus inviting all to enter
Who would flee from dire destruction,
Offering all who came within it,
Food and shelter all they needed,
Freely as the air of heaven.
　Thus it is the loving Saviour
Stands with open arms to welcome
All whose eyes have once been opened
To behold their guilt and danger,
And the death that sure awaits them,
If in Him they are not sheltered
From the Law's just retribution.
　Though these cities only offered
Welcome refuge to the *guiltless*,
Who had not with fixed intention
Caused the death of human beings,
But who by some chance had slain them,
Yet our Saviour stands with pity,
Full of love and of compassion,
Ready to receive the *guilty*,
Who, alas! have often broken
Holy laws in mercy given
For the good of all God's creatures.
　Yes, the loving Saviour offers
Free forgiveness to the guilty,
Telling them that He has suffered
For the sins they have committed,
That if they will only trust Him,

He will most securely shield them
From the Law's avenging fury,
So that they may always safely
Bask beneath His smiling favour,
And in Him find every blessing
Here and in the great Hereafter.

    Reader, are you safe in Jesus?
Have you fled to Him for refuge?
Is the law against you silenced,
Threatening nought of dreadful vengeance
For your sins against high heaven?

    Have you really been awakened?
Have you seen your awful danger
While afar from Christ you linger?

    Oh, how can you longer tarry
When you have so free a welcome
Offered to you by the Saviour,
Shielding you from every danger,
Filling up your heart with gladness?

    Of this be assured, my reader,
On your track is the avenger,
Tho' you may not now believe it,
He will one day overtake you,
While you sleep He will not tarry.

    Justice walks with leaden sandals,
But with iron hand he striketh
Sinners out of Christ the Refuge.

    O then flee at once for safety
To the Saviour who is waiting,
Standing with His hands uplifted,—
Hands that once for you were piercèd
By the nails upon Mount Calvary,
Calling, pleading, 'Come, thou guilty,
I am still the Friend of sinners,
I will shield thee from the vengeance
Of the law which thou hast broken.'

Now, methinks I hear thee saying,
'I will flee at once to Jesus,
Well I know that I am guilty,
God's laws I have often broken,
Often scorned His gracious message,
Offering pardon to me freely.
Often, Saviour, thou hast called me,
But I did not know my danger;
Did not know my need of refuge;
Did not see the fierce avenger,
Which upon my track was hastening.
But since Thou hast suffered for me,
I may trust in Thee for pardon.
Dearest Saviour, just now take me,
Take me to Thy loving bosom,
Clasp me in Thy warm affections,
As I am I now come to Thee,
Tears will never make me better,
'Tis Thy blood alone that cleanseth
All my sins away for ever.
Thus, Thou loving Jesus, take me,
Make me Thine, yes, Thine for ever.'
Then with joy I shall be singing :—

Looking only to Jesus, the Crucified One,
Who invites all that mourn; will you come? will you come?
I have left all my sins at the foot of the cross;
Sinful pleasures are now to my taste but as dross.

Oh, how oft have I heard of the Saviour who died,
That my fears might be quelled, and my tears all be dried;

But alas! my proud heart was too stubborn to
    yield,
To his kind invitation to come and be healed.

But at length God in mercy has led me to see,
That if I would find safety to Christ I must flee;
The avenger of blood I have seen on my track,
But with Jesus my refuge I'll never turn back.

Still to Jesus I'll look, though life's journey be
    long;
When approaching the river let this be my song:
All my sins washed away in the *peace-speaking
    blood*,
Come, dear Jesus, come quickly, and take me
    to God.

CHAPTER VIII.

AFTER visiting the ruins
 Of a synagogue at Kedesh,
  Massive ruins, grand, majestic,
Speaking of the former grandeur
Of the city God appointed
As a refuge for man-slayers,—
Then they turned their steps to Safed.
Long and weary was the day's ride,
Up high mountains, down deep valleys,
But the scenery, so majestic,
More than paid them for their trouble.
 On their left they passed by Hazor,
Where once lived the wicked Jabin,
Who was leader of the armies
Met at Merom's bitter waters,
And who there with all his allies
Fell before the hosts of Israel.
 Not a house they found where Hazor
Stood three thousand years now by-gone.
 While the sun was gently sinking
To his couch all decked with crimson,
Lighting up the distant hill-tops
With a gleam of heavenly brightness,
Then it was that they ascended
To the very top of Safed,

Where the hill is crowned with ruins
Of an old Crusader Castle.
　O how glorious and how lovely
Was the **prospect** then before them.
　First of all their eyes were feasted,
Gazing long upon the Lake of
Galilee which lay before them.
　Ne'er will they forget their feelings
While they gazed upon those waters,
Sacred with the name of Jesus.
　To the east were Hauron's Mountains,
Stretching from the banks of Jordan
Into the Arabian desert,
Where once dwelt the King of Bashan,
Og by name, that mighty giant
Who slept on a bed of iron
Fully twelve long feet in measure.
　To the west the range of Carmel
Pressed its way toward the sea-shore.
Just beyond they saw there resting,
Sleeping like a mighty giant,
Waters of the Mediterranean.
　All around were many objects
Filled with interest to the readers
Of the precious Holy Bible;
But the sea where Jesus tarried,
Where he preached so oft the Gospel,
Where He chose His own disciples,
Where he made them to be fishers,
With the Gospel net, for sinners,
Where He dwelt in ' His own city,'
Where He raisèd Jairus' daughter,
On whose banks he fed five thousand;
There around those sacred waters
Their chief interest was centred.
　So clear was the air of heaven

That the lake seemed but a stone's-throw
From the place where they were standing,
Though it was full ten miles distant.
   The next morn the sun rose glorious,
Lighting up the lake and valley,
Making all things bright and lovely.
   Though they knew the Jews considered
Safed as a holy city,
Still they found there nought of interest
To detain them on their journey.
   Thus, whene'er the word was given,
Stars and Stripes, our nation's banner,
Then no longer floated o'er them,
Tents were struck, and packed all closely
Into sacks on beasts of burden.
   Down the steep and rugged footpath
Michael led, and quickly followed
Seventeen laden mules and horses,
All belonging to the party.
   Oft they stopped and gathered flowers,
Lovely flowers by the wayside,
Tho' it was almost December.
   Once they passed a den where robbers
Live, 'tis said, far 'neath the mountain.
   Finally at Ain-et-Tiny,
'Fountain of the fig,' they halted,
Thought by some to be Capernaum.
A great rock them offered shelter
From the sun, who was too fervent
In his warm addresses to them.
   All around were oleanders,
Blooming lovely in the sunlight,
Also there they found Papyrus,
Which was once made into paper,
Yes, from which that name was taken.
   Ducks were swimming in the fountain,

But a stone's-throw from the waters,
'Side which Jesus fed five thousand.
　After lunch again they mounted,
Down they galloped by the sea-shore,
Close by where the waters ripple,
Oft coquetting with the sea-shells,
Which, like youthful maidens, linger
For their oft repeated visit.
　In an hour or two they entered
Magdala, the home of Mary,
From whom Jesus cast seven devils.
Now, alas! it is a village
Of mud huts, and few in number;
Still we felt a tender interest,
As we knew that we were standing
Where that woman oft had wandered.
　'Tis no wonder that she loved much,
Having been so much forgiven.
　Having laved their limbs so weary
In the hot baths of Tiberias,—
Fahrenheit one hundred forty,
Bursting from volcanic mountains,
Where the red-hot fires are burning,
As in days when wrote Josephus,
They sat down beneath their tentings,
Close beside the placid waters
Of the lake oft called Gennesareth.
　There, while gazing on the waters,
And upon the lovely landscape,
Edward wrote this in his note-book :—

Beneath Tiberias' ancient wall,
　We pitched our tents on Galilee,
Just as the sunbeams ceased to fall
　Across the silent deep blue sea.

Ere long the clear full moon appeared,
  And bridged the lake with her bright beams;
But to our hearts all was endeared,
  Because that here were Bible scenes.

'Twas on that very lake we knew
  Our blessed Saviour walked at will;
When waves rolled high, and fierce winds blew,
  'Twas by His word He made them still.

How wonderful it is to gaze
  Upon this lake where Christ has been;
It makes us live in other days:
  The flood and ruins speak of Him.

This day we rode along the shore,
  From where once stood Capernaum;
Alas! alas! it is no more!
  Upon its ruins shines the sun.

We thought of how the Saviour there,
  In 'His own city' preached the Word;
And how they came from everywhere,
  And from His lips the gospel heard.

How sad it was for us to think,
  That city once exalted high,
Was cast down to perdition's brink,
  Because they heeded not His cry.

We gathered shells along the beach,
    To take to friends across the sea;
For well we knew that they would each
    Prize something from dear Galilee.

We thought of how the fishermen,
    From night till morn had toiled for nought;
Let down their nets once and again,
    And yet, alas! had nothing caught!

We seemed to see our Saviour stand
    Close by the ship, and say at dawn,
'Let down the nets at my command,
    And many fishes shall be drawn.'

We could but offer up the prayer,
    'Lord, when we cast the gospel net,
Then may we feel thy presence there,
    That it may not in vain be set.'

Thus, as we walk by Galilee,
    Where when on earth, Lord, Thou didst dwell,
May every thought be turned to Thee,
    And every tongue Thy glory tell.

    Beaming in the morning sunlight,
Calm and peaceful lay the waters,
In the bosom of the mountains,
Gentle as a child in slumber,
Winning all still closer to them.

Ere long they were on its surface,
With the Arabs—O how ignorant
Of the art of navigation !
What then followed, Edward tells you
In some lines he wrote, when turning
Back from crossing to Bethsaida.
They are truthful in their statements :—

We started for Bethsaida,
　On board a little, crazy ship;
The distance seemed not very far,
　And o'er the waves we hoped to skip.

When we were out a little way,
　The Doctor of our party said,
'I hope we'll have a storm to-day,'
　Then turned him to his book and read.

Then from Mount Hermon's lofty height,
　And from the hills of Naphtali,
Fierce clouds soon burst upon our sight,
　And swept the sea of Galilee.

Its placid waters soon were tossed
　In foaming billows all around;—
In vain we wished the sea were crossed,
　And we were on the solid ground.

The billows rolled, the wind was high,
　And every heart was anxious ; then
We prayed, 'O Saviour ! come Thou nigh,
　And still the waters once again !'

The Saviour heard our pleading cry,
    And quickly stilled our wild alarm;
We felt that He indeed drew nigh,
    For suddenly the sea was calm.

'Twas then we felt the Saviour near,
    As did His followers on that sea.
He from our hearts had banished fear,
    And quelled the waves of Galilee.

Dear Saviour, may we always feel
    That Thou art never far away;
But that, wherever we may kneel,
    There Thou art with us when we pray.

CHAPTER IX.

THOUGH the storm, so unexpected,
  Drove them back from whence they
    started,
They were not the less determined
They would see the sacred places
Near to which the Jordan mingles
With the lake its turbid waters.
  Many ruins claimed their interest,
Marking where once stood the cities
Into which Christ often entered,
Preaching words of deepest meaning.
  Long they halted at Capernaum—
Tell-Hum now the Arabs call it,
Recent excavations prove it—
Rather than at Ain-et-Tiny.
  There they saw the massive ruins
Of a synagogue, upon which
Jesus' feet must oft have rested.
'Tis on earth the only pavement
Upon which 'tis known, with surety,
Christ our Lord hath surely trodden.
  Beautiful Corinthian columns
There lay prostrate in the rubbish.
Would that they could but have told them
Of the words they had heard spoken
From the lips of Christ our Saviour!

Wandering there among the ruins,
They perchance trod where Jairus
Often, with his little daughter,
Hand in hand once walked together.
 And perchance they sat and rested
On the stones which formed his mansion,
In which Jesus raised his daughter,
Snatching her from Death's embraces,
Giving her back to her parents.
Ah! how often must the Saviour,
As He walked in ' His own city,'[1]
Have been gladdened with the footfall
Of that dear one running to Him,
With a brow on which twelve summers
There had painted rosebud beauty!
 Happy child, thus to have taken
Jesus' hand in her embraces,
Printing oft upon it kisses,
While, with heart all full of gladness,
Oft she told Him how she loved Him
For His loving-kindness to her.
 She well knew He loved the children,
That He never would repulse her.
She, no doubt, too, heard Him saying,
Let the little children gather
Round me, for they know I love them—
Let them come and get my blessing—
Up in heaven I wish to meet them,
Where there are so many gathered,
And where all who wish to enter
Must come humbly, like the children,
With their docile disposition.
 Doubtless she oft brought her playmates
To her dear-loved Friend and Saviour,
Telling them that He could make them

[1] Matt. ix. 1, and xviii. 27.

Happy, if they would but trust Him;
That He would their sins forgive them,
And a new heart put within them,
And thus fit them for the glories
Of His home far up in heaven.
We could almost hear her singing :—

    Blessed Jesus, how I love thee!
        Thou hast snatched me from the grave,
    I will evermore adore Thee,
        For Thy wondrous power to save.

    Cold I lay in death's embraces,
        Hence the vital spark had fled;
    Thou of life couldst see no traces,
        I was numbered with the dead.

    Yet Thy mighty word hath raised me,
        Brought the colour to my cheek,
    Thou, O Lord, from death hath saved me,
        Of Thy praises I will speak.

    Yes, this tongue that once was silent,
        Ne'er shall cease to tell Thy love;
    Praise shall now be its employment,
        Here on earth and up above.

    Tho' a *child* within this city,
        Yet Thou didst not pass me by,
    Thou for me didst show such pity,
        That for Thee I now could die.

O how changed my heart is toward thee !
    Once I never loved Thy name ;
With the wicked I oft scorned Thee,
    At the thought I blush with shame.

Now whenever I must listen
    To a word toward Thee unkind,
In my eyes the tears will glisten,
    And a cloud come o'er my mind.

I will bring to get Thy blessing
    All the children that I can ;
They near Thee will soon be pressing,
    Unless pushed away by man.

If they only will but pray Thee,
    Thou wilt listen to their prayer.
Jesus, let not Satan slay me,
    Make us all Thy constant care.

    Near Capernaum they noticed
A small harbour, where once anchored
Peter, James, and John their vessels,
After weary hours of fishing.
    There, or near that spot, our Saviour
Called them from their occupation.
' Follow Me, and I will make you
Of mankind e'en to be fishers,
With the net of My providing.'
O how blessed is the record—
' Straight they left their nets and followed
Him, who henceforth was their Master.'

My dear reader, Christ is calling,
Bidding you walk in His footsteps.
'Follow Me' is His injunction,
Listen to Him, He will bless you;
O delay not, lest He leave you.
You'll be happy in His service,
All your sins He will forgive you,
He will fit you for His kingdom.
Faithful unto death,—He'll give you
Crown of life and joys unending.

His disciples quickly followed,
Tho' He then had not been wounded
For the sins they had committed.

But to you He shows the places
Where the nails His hands have piercèd;
Points you to His brow, all bleeding,
Crying, Look to Me, poor sinner,
'Twas for thee all this I suffered,
'Twas for all of thy transgressions
That I bled on Calvary's mountain.

O how can you then but trust Him?
Is your heart too hard to love Him?
Sure 'tis like the nether millstone,
If you can resist such pleadings.

CHAPTER X.

THEY would fain have longer tarried
At the site of old Chorazin
And Bethsaida, the cities
Cursed of God for their rejecting
Christ their Lord, whose work so mighty
Should have led them all to trust Him.
But where once were teeming thousands,
'Multitudes' beyond all number,
Now, alas! are plundering Arabs,
Ready to waylay the traveller,
After nightfall, on their borders.

   So they turned back to Tiberias,
Keeping close beside the waters
Of the sacred sea so lovely.

   As they passed by Ain-et-Tiny,
There they gathered the papyrus,
Which in all of Palestina
There alone can be seen growing.
Once it grew in far-off Egypt.

   Finally, again they rested
At Tiberias 'neath their tenting.

   As the sun next morn was rising,
They were up and eating breakfast
'Neath the canopy of heaven,
Altho' it was in December,
Near its close, but yet the weather
Was like a New England May-day.

O how soft and how delicious
Was the balmy air that morning!
　After going through the city
Built by Herod, he who murdered
John the Baptist, for Herodias,
All because she danced to please him,
Then they sadly turned their faces
Up the hill, or rather mountain,
Where 'tis said Christ preached His sermon,
With the mountain for His pulpit,
And His sounding-board, the heavens.
　On that sacred place they lingered,
Glorious was the view afforded
On all sides from that high eminence.
　While the ladies there were gathering
Flowers to press in their herbarium,
Edward quickly wrote the following :—

Farewell, farewell, a long, a last farewell,
　　Dear lovely Galilee;
Our Lord upon thy borders loved to dwell,
　　Thy name is dear to me.

How quickly have the days and hours flown past,
　　Which we have spent by thee;
From Hattin's Mount our last fond look we cast
　　On thee, dear Galilee.

'Twas from this brow our Saviour preached, 'tis said,
　　His sermon on the mount,
'Twas yonder that the multitude were fed
　　In numbers none could count.

And thou didst mirror all this wondrous scene,
  O Sea of Galilee!
Couldst thou but speak and tell all thou hast seen,
  How happy we should be.

Of doomed Bethsaida thou sure wouldst tell,
  And of Capernaum;
How they were cast from heaven down to hell,
  For hating God's own Son.

But thou wouldst oftener speak of Christ our Lord,
  Who walked upon the beach;
And thou wouldst tell how to the multitude
  He plainly there did preach.

Yet wondrous tales to us thou'st had to tell,
  O Sea of Galilee!
Now we must say a long, a last farewell,
  We turn for aye from thee!

CHAPTER XI.

 FEW hours from Hattin's Mountain
Brought them to the place where Jesus
Graced the marriage feast of Cana,[1]
Where His mother and relations
Saw the miracle so wondrous,
By which water-pots of water,
At the mighty word of Jesus,
Quick were filled with wine delicious.
 They were shown three of those vessels,
Which the monks, with much assurance,
Told them once were at the marriage
Spoken of within the Bible.
 On they hastened quick to Nazareth ;
O how lovely was the prospect,
When at length it burst upon them
At the peaceful hour of sunset !
 'There,' they said, 'the Holy Jesus
Lived and toiled, "a man of sorrows,"
There in all points like us tempted,
With His dear-loved mother, Mary,
Subject oft, no doubt, to trials
From the scoffing Jews about Him.'
 Yet without one word of murmur,
There within that lovely valley,
Clothed with flesh, once dwelt the Saviour,

[1] John ii. 1-12.

He of worlds the mighty Maker,
Who for our sake took our nature,
And to death became obedient,
That we might be saved from dying,
And might live with Him in heaven,
Where all tears are wiped for ever
From the eyes of God's dear children.
  It was there He was rejected[1]
By His townsmen, whom with blessing
He most gladly would have loaded,
If they would His word have heeded.
  Messianic psalms they thought of;
Of His words so full of sorrow;
They could almost hear Him saying,
'To my brethren I'm a stranger,
From my mother's children alien;
My soul is consumed in fasting;
Shame, alas, my face has covered.'[2]
  After He had been accepted
By His Father at the Jordan,
When a voice came from high heaven,
'This my Son is my beloved;'—
Oh! how sad to be rejected
By the wicked men of Nazareth.
  With such thoughts they entered Nazareth,
Soon were at the Latin convent,
Wearied with their eight hours' riding.
  Many were the objects shown them,
While they lingered there in Nazareth,
With which they were told that Jesus
When He lived there was familiar;
They were taken to the work-shop,
And were told He there was subject
To His parents at their bidding;—

---

[1] Luke iv. 29. [2] Psalm lxix. 7-20.

To the place of annunciation,
Where the angel spoke to Mary,
So 'tis said by long tradition,
When she heard that she was favoured,
'And that she should be the mother
Of the holy child called Jesus,'[1]
To the rock called Mensa Christa,
Which, they say, with His disciples,
Once our Lord used for a table
After He from death had risen.
To the high brow of the mountain,
Where the angry people led Him,
And from whence they would have thrust Him
For his faithful words unto them;[2]
To those places and to others
They were taken, while in Nazareth,
Though about them they were doubtful.

One place was to them most real,
'Twas the fountain of the village,
To which Jesus oft resorted,
In his days of youth and manhood.

Back of Nazareth there riseth,
As of old a lofty hill-top
On which Christ must oft have wandered.

There, no doubt, He oft communed with
God His Father, of His mission
To a world by sin all ruined.

'T is no wonder that the travellers
Were delighted with their visit
To this eminence, which rises
High above the vale of Nazareth.

To the west they saw Mount Carmel,[3]
Saw the Spot where once the altar,
With the bullock laid upon it,

[1] Luke i. 28.   [2] Luke iv. 29.   [3] 1 Kings xviii. 19-40.

With its trench all filled with water,
Was consumed with holy fire,
After that the good Elijah,
Seeing that all Baal's prophets
Could do nought with their enchantments,
With his prayer called down from heaven
Holy fire, which burnt the sacrifice,
Yes, and 'licked up' all the water.
   'Twas no wonder that the people
Quickly then fell on their faces,
Crying yes, O yes we'll worship
God the Lord, but never Baal.
   There before them was the river,
Kishon called, that 'ancient river,'
Where Elijah slew the prophets,
Numbering four hundred fifty.
   Ere they left the home of Jesus,
Edward wrote these lines about it:—

  Tell me, did the Saviour dwell
     Thirty years upon this site?
  Did He on this lovely dell,
     Often look at morn and night?

  Yes, O yes, this was His home,
     Here it was His life was spent,
  He did thro' this valley roam,
     O'er these hills He often went.

  'Twas from yonder hill He gazed
     On the snowy Lebanon,
  There He also often traced
     Carmel gilded with the sun.

Subject to His parents' will,
   Here He toiled the livelong day,
Thinking of His mission still,
   Of His home so far away.

At that fountain slaked His thirst,
   With his mother by His side,—
'Tis the only one that bursts
   Out from all the green hillside.

From this city He was cast
   Fiercely to yon mountain's brow,
But He quickly through them passed,
   In a way they knew not how.

For His townsmen long He yearned,
   Longed to see them holy men,
But their anger toward Him burned
   For His faithfulness to them.

Dearest Saviour, make me Thine,
   Help me follow in Thy way,
Though I suffer for a time
   Thou wilt wipe my tears away.

CHAPTER XII.

TABOR claimed their next attention,
Passing east right through the valley,
Where were many flowers, fragrant,
Like the ones that Jesus gathered.
Then ascended they the hill-top,
One of thirteen that now guardeth,—
Couchant-like, the home of Mary,
From its top they saw Mount Tabor,[1]
Thickly wooded with the terabinth.
Lovely in its every aspect.
  Finally they reached its summit,
In its lofty isolations.
  It reminded them of Rigi,
Which looks down upon Lake Zurich.
  There they saw the great Esdraelon,
Stretching far and wide its grass fields,
Where for ages mighty battles
Have been fought with direst carnage.
  From that mountain-top descended
To that valley, with ten thousand,
Barak and the heroine Deborah,
Driving hence the iron chariots,
Full nine hundred was their number,
Of that wicked captain Sisera,
Who was sent away from Hazor
By the heathen king called Jabin,

[1] Judges iv. 6.

To subdue the hosts of Israel.
God was with His servant Barak,
Thus his enemies were conquered.
There it was the great Napoleon,
With his band of but three thousand,
Fought the Turks, full thirty thousand,
Driving them from their position,
Yea, defeating them completely.
  Tho' from Tabor 'twas some distance,
Still 'tis called 'Mount Tabor's' battle.
  On the summit of that mountain
They were taken to a convent,
Where six men, who looked like hermits,
Round an altar highly tinselled,
Stood and sang, or rather chanted
With a nasal twang their jargon,

   Idra, idra, ino, no !
   Idra, idra, ino, no !

To their idol, Virgin Mary.
  On its walls were many paintings
Of our Lord's transfiguration,
Which they claim was on that mountain,
Tho' 'tis plain to every student,
That upon some spur of Hermon,
That scene must have been located.
  None till after the fourth century
Speak of Tabor as the mountain
Where our Lord was once transfigured.
At that time 'tis known with surety,
That 'twas covered o'er with dwellings,
Thus preventing that seclusion,
Which was sought for by our Saviour,
When He would to His disciples
Show that He was more than human,

Yea, that He was God incarnate.
Nought is seen there now but ruins,
Very massive in their structure,
Beasts of prey their only tenants.

  The next day the party started
For Jennin, their next encampment.
They had heard so much of robbers,
That their Dragoman most cautious
Orders gave to keep together,
That the cavalcade might frighten
Prowling Bedwins seeking plunder.
  On their left they passed the lofty
'Mountain of precipitation,'
Where some falsely claim that Jesus
Once was dragged by His own townsmen,
That they might in fiercest anger
Cast him headlong from its summit.
  Travelling on an hour from Nazareth,
They approached the very village [1]
Where the Saviour in compassion
Filled with joy the weeping widow,
Who, from Nain, the populous city,
To the sepulchre was going
With her son to see him buried.
  Oft their thoughts by scenes around them
Had been led to think of battles
Where grim death cut down his thousands.
Now, how pleasant 'twas to think of
One who came with loving-kindness,
Armed with mighty power from Heaven,
Able to restore the dying,
Yea, to call the dead to being.
  What a scene was then enacted,
When the word of Christ was spoken,

[1] Luke vii. 11.

And that mother clasped her offspring,
Pressing close his lips so fondly;
How they must have clung to Jesus,
Loading Him with benedictions,
Promising that they would always
Serve Him for His loving-kindness.

 Farther to the left lay Endor [1]
At the foot of 'Little Hermon,'
Where King Saul had once consulted
One who had an evil spirit,
At whose word the prophet Samuel
Came to Saul with words of warning,
Telling him that on the morrow,
Rent from him should be the kingdom,
That he also should be numbered
With his sons among the wounded,
Or with them he should be sleeping
That long sleep that knows no waking.

 Rounding the west end of Hermon,
Right before them they saw Shunem, [2]
With its orange groves so luscious,
And its lemons in abundance.

 Oh! how different are its people,
From the time when Great King David
Sent there for his wife Abishag,—
She, the lovely, fairest damsel
'Throughout all the coast of Israel.'

 Now, within their wretched hovels,
They saw none the least attractive.

 Oft they wondered where the house stood
Where Elisha sometimes tarried
In the room which was built for him,
Where there stood a 'bed and table,'
And the little things he needed.

 Then they thought of how the prophet

---

[1] 1 Sam. xxviii. 7   [2] 2 Kings iv. 8-10.

In that room called back to being
The loved child of that good woman,
Who to him had shown such kindness.
  Oh ! how joyous was that mother
When a second time was sent her,
From the Lord her boy beloved—
All because of hospitality
Shown to one of God's dear servants,
Who had power to call down blessing
From his heavenly Father's storehouse.
  Through the plain of Esdraelon,
O'er the battle-field of ages,
After a few miles of riding,
They approached the 'Well of trembling,'[1]
In the Bible called 'Ain Harod,'
All because that there the fearful
Were by Gideon exhorted
To return from the great battle,
Which they feared with so much trembling.
  Then it was full twenty thousand
Fled from the approaching Bedwins,
For the Lord would have the glory,
Lest they say, 'our own hand saved us.'[2]
  Then it was the fearless Gideon,
Upon whom the Spirit rested,
Did as God had him commanded,
And with his three hundred tried ones,
At the silent hour of midnight,
Gathered round the hosts of Midian,
And when once they saw the signal,
Blew their trumpets, brake their pitchers,
Shouting loud with all their voices,
' 'Tis the sword of God and Gideon.'
  Then it was they quickly routed
All the mighty hosts of Midian,

[1] Judges vii. 1-5.   [2] Judges vii. 2.

So that in their blinded fury
They drew swords against each other,
Slaying thousands of their kindred.
   At the well when the three hundred
Lapped like dogs before the battle,
There the pilgrims drank the water,
Which still flows as fresh as ever.
   'Tis a large and lovely fountain,
As a lake in its appearance.
   Gladly also did their horses
Cool their dusty limbs within it.
   Now three thousand years have passed since
At this fountain of Jezreel,
That event occurred which made it
Famous throughout all the ages.
Still they seemed to hear its waters
Saying to them, 'Be not fearful,'—
Trust in God in every battle,
Fear not foes, tho' they be mighty,
Numerous as the swarming locusts,
Tho' be with you but three hundred,
And your enemies three thousand,
Yet if God is ever with you,
And you sound aloud the watchword,
'"Tis the sword of God and Gideon,'
Then o'er all you soon shall triumph,
Yes, and then you'll be like Gideon,
Sometimes 'faint, but yet pursuing."[1]

[1] Judges viii. 4.

CHAPTER XIII.

TURNING to the west, the pilgrims
   Then ascended to the summit
   Of the hill where stood the city,
On which rose the royal palace
Of King Ahab, king of Israel.
   As they wandered o'er the ruins,
Where was once the royal city,
Which by Jezebel was governed—
Oft their thoughts turned to that woman,
She of Sidon's king the daughter,
Wily, crafty, domineering,
Yet, who finally was baffled
By the God whom she offended.
   As they wandered round the hill-top,
Fancy it once more repeopled—
'Here,' they said, 'was Naboth's vineyard,
Coveted by wicked Ahab,
For whose sake his queen did murder
Naboth—he, its lawful owner.'
'Here,' they said, 'perchance the palace
Out from which was thrown that woman
At the word of valiant Jehu;
These perhaps the stones that crushed her,
When she fell from that high window
Down upon the hard stone pavement.'
   And these canines, which are barking,

May be some of the descendants
Of the dogs which ate up Jezebel.[1]
   Who would not to-day the rather
Bear the name of murdered Naboth?
Is not Naboth envied rather
Than the wicked King of Israel,
And his wife the blood-stained Jezebel?
   May their history prove a warning.
If, alas! we e'er are tempted
By allurements which sin offers,
May we stop and think of Jezebel,
And the God who sure will punish
All who break His laws so holy.
   Thus they talked, and thus reflected,
While at Ahab's court they lingered.
   Finally, from that high out-look,
Where had often walked Elijah,
Sad they turned away their faces
From the glorious prospect northward.
   Leaving on their left Gilboa,
Speaking to them of the battle,
In which Saul, the mighty, perished,
On the travellers passed to Jennin,
Thinking of that lamentation,
Uttered by the royal Psalmist,
At the death of Saul and Jon'than,
By the hands of the Philistines.
   Lovely was their ride to Jennin,
On that warm November morning,
All day long they had been riding
O'er the plain of Esdraelon.
   For some miles they quickly galloped
O'er that tract so smooth and level,
For they knew that on the morrow
Rocks, and stones, and rugged mountains
Would full oft retard their progress.

[1] 2 Kings ix. 10.

En-gannim, it's named quite truly,
For, e'en now the lovely gardens
And its bright and sparkling fountains,
Hedges of the pear so prickly,
All conspire to make it lovely.
   But, alas! the wretched people
Sadly contrast with the scenery,
For they are a set of robbers.
All night long poor Michael sat up
To protect their camp from plunder,
Yet upon their hair mattrasses,
Placed upon the iron bedsteads,
Sound they slept, by God protected,
Saying, as they closed their eyelids,
' Peaceful we'll lay down to slumber,
Thou alone canst keep us safely.'[1]
   When the morning sun was rising,
They were up and eating breakfast
'Neath the canopy of heaven,
While the tents were being loaded
On their mules and beasts of burden.
   After a few hours of riding,
They approached the site of Dothan,[2]
Where poor Joseph found his brethren,
And where he was sold so basely
To the Ishmaelites, who journeyed
Then as now, across that valley,
On their way from Jabesh-Gilead
To the far-off land of Egypt,
With their camels bearing spices,
Balm and myrrh to sell to Pharaoh.
   Oh! how true that God oft causes
Wrath of man to turn to praises.
   But while strolling about Dothan,[3]
They were often led to think of
How Ben-hadad sent to capture

---

[1] Psalm iv. 8.   [2] Gen. xxxvii. 17-20.   [3] Gen. xxxvii. 17.

The good prophet, bold Elisha,
All because that by his knowledge
He oft thwarted Syria's armies,
While they sought to take Samaria.
' Here,' they said, was where the servant
Saw the horses and the chariots
Of Ben-hadad's mighty army,—
Here, that he became so frightened
Crying out, our case is hopeless,
Here it was he heard the answer,
Fear not, for there are more with us
Than with them—for God is with us.
   Here, upon this very hill-top,
Quick Elisha's[1] prayer was answered,
And the young man's eyes were opened
To behold the flaming horses,
With the glittering fiery chariot.
   While they talked thus, and reflected
On the scenes at Dothan acted,
Oh ! how could these Christian travellers
Help but trust in God more fully,
Firm resolving they would never
Murmur, tho' like Joseph treated,
Yea, that they would never falter,
Tho' by mighty hosts surrounded,
But the rather like Elisha,
Pray the Lord their eyes to open,
Showing them that He was mighty
To defend them from all danger,—
Yea, that when from earth departing,
They might find their bed as Dothan,
All surrounded with bright angels,
Ready, quick to bear them heavenward,
Far beyond the reach of Satan,
Where no enemy shall enter,
There, with Joseph and Elisha,

[1] 2 Kings vi. 13.

And with all the holy angels,
Praising God for all His mercies.

   Leaving Dothan, then they followed
In the footsteps of Elisha,
When he led Ben-hadad's servants,
Blinded, back unto Samaria,
Where they looked for nought but slaughter
   On their right they saw a mountain,
To which Edward quickly galloped,
Leaving Ida and the party
Following the guide in safety.
   From that high, majestic outlook,
Edward saw the Mediterranean,
Also gazed upon the ruins,
Desolate and uninhabited,
Where once stood proud Cæsarea.
   Just a little before sunset,
After passing many places
Noted in the Bible history,
They caught sight of that high hill-top,
Which was once crowned with Samaria,
Where once dwelt the Kings of Israel,
After it had rivalled Tirzah,
And become the royal city.
   From that hill where stood Samaria,
On all sides the view was glorious
At that quiet hour of sunset.
   Like some vast impregnable fortress,
On each side with moat surrounded,
Rose that isolated mountain,
Which Ben-hadad[1] sought to capture.
   What a sight must have been witnessed,
When within that wallèd city,
Famine stalked abroad so ghastly,
Slaying rich and poor together,

[1] 1 Kings xx. 10.

Driving mothers well nigh frantic,
Till at last they ate their children.
Then it was the king in madness
Charged it all upon Elisha,
Saying he should be beheaded—
But he from the holy prophet
Heard that flour upon the morrow
Should be plenty in Samaria.

That same night four starving lepers,[1]
Who without the gate were staying,
In a fit of desperation,
Rose and fled unto the Syrians,
Thinking, tho' their dreaded enemies,
They perchance would show compassion,
And would satisfy their hunger.
How amazed were they to find that
All the Syrians had departed
In great fright from their encampment,
Leaving *food*, and *gold*, and *raiment*
In abundance for the lepers,
Yea, enough for all Samaria,
So that soon all in the city
Were with richest store made happy;
And the word Elisha uttered
Was made good unto the letter.

One there was who saw the blessing,
But had been so unbelieving,
God in judgment it so ordered
That he by the hungry people,
As they thro' the gateway hurried,
Was trod under, thus he perished.

While among Samaria's ruins
Thus they learned important lessons,
Vividly impressed upon them.

How like sinners seemed those lepers,
Wretched, hungry, starving, dying,

[1] 2 Kings vii. 3.

Fearing much themselves to venture,
Where was nought but life and riches.
   Just so, many venture slowly
To the Saviour, who has offered
Life and *wealth* and *every blessing*,
Without money, all so freely.
Many think that He will rob them
Of their numerous, joyous pleasures—
Thus an *enemy* they call Him.
   While in passing, may I ask you,
Have *you* found in Christ the treasures
Which to you, dear friend, He offers?
He will give you *bread* from heaven,
Bread that satisfies for ever.
He will give you *gold* that's precious,
Which will make you rich most truly,
He will *clothe* you with that garment,
Which all wear, who enter heaven,
Yea, His righteousness He'll give you,
You will find in Him a 'friend that
Sticketh closer than a brother'—
Yea, the 'chiefest of ten thousands,
And the altogether lovely'—
He will fill your heart with pleasures,
To which you have been a stranger.
   Think of how much blood it cost Him,
Of the groans, and of the sorrow,
Of the bloody sweat and suffering,
Of the cruel crown and mockings,
Of the cross with all its torture,
He endured to buy these treasures,
Which He offers to enrich you,
Here in time, and up in heaven.
Oh! then, go to Him this hour,
He'll receive you—He'll forgive you—
Only trust Him, you will love Him.

Like that lord so unbelieving,
Do not perish in the sight of
Food and wealth, and life eternal.
  Rather be like those Samaritans,
Who, in days long after Ahab,
Listened to the precious Gospel
In such numbers, that Samaria,
All with one accord attentive,
Was made happy by the tidings;[1]
So that then within that city
There were very great rejoicings.
  If, like them, *you* would be happy,
You must flee to Christ the Saviour.
  Brightly rose the sun that morning,
Lighting up the lofty hill-top,
Where in later years King Herod
Built the city called Sabastia—
Naming it from proud Augustus,
Who had given Him the city.
Thus 'twas called when the Evangelist
Philip there proclaimed the Gospel,
Planting there a branch of Zion.
Ah! how changed are now the people,
All night long poor Michael watched them,
Lighting up his camp-fire often,
Lest by force they come for plunder.
  As the party passed their houses,
At them they threw stones most rudely;
Yes, and one of them struck Ida.
Mrs. B. was much astonished
When she found within her pocket
Some one's hand, to her a stranger.
  Now, alas! the sad predictions[2]
Uttered by the holy prophets,
Threatening death to proud Samaria,
Are fulfilled unto the letter.

[1] Acts viii. 8.   [2] Micah i. 6.

Grass is growing where were temples,
And the feet of prancing horses.
Down the hill-side to the valley,
Columns, once all smoothly polished,
Had been tumbled by the ploughman.
  Thus as God once spoke by Micah,
E'en the stones are in the valley,
Which were once in grand old houses.
  Sixty columns still are standing,
Each one now decapitated,
Which once formed a lofty archway
From the arch of triumph, reaching
To the palace of King Herod.
Now, alas! they weep in silence
O'er the glory long departed.
Ne'er again shall mighty chariots
Waken echoes in their presence.
And the dance of young Salome,
Daughter of the vain Herodias,
Causing death to John the Baptist,
Ne'er again will be repeated.
Now none ask where they were buried,
Who beheaded that bold preacher;
But upon that very hill-top
Travellers always seek to visit
The old church of *John the Baptist*,
Where, with ruins most imposing,
Rests the body of that martyr—
This, at least, is the tradition.
  Oh! how true that persecution
Oft exalts the weak and suffering,
E'en to *earthly* fame and glory,
While as centuries roll onward,
Those who hated them so fiercely
Are forgotten or detested.

CHAPTER XIV.

NOT a place in Palestina
Rivals in its situation
Shechem, between Mount Gerizim
And Mount Ebal, tow'ring lofty.
To that valley, all so verdant,
With its lovely, charming fountains,
Sparkling in the light of heaven,
Came the travellers from Samaria,
As the morning sun was pouring
Golden light on hill and valley.
After riding through the city,
Through its streets so very narrow,
Filled with followers of the Prophet,
Numbering at least seven thousand,
Full of hatred to the Christians,
Often heaping on them insult,
They approached the tomb of Joseph,[1]
At the entrance of the valley,
Between Ebal and Gerizim.
Strange to say, the Moslems claim it,
This the rather but confirms it
As the real tomb of Joseph.
Nought is seen but an enclosure,
Which itself is doubtless modern;
But within it all agree that
Dust of Joseph now reposes.

[1] Joshua xxiv. 32.

God's Word tells us that to Shechem
Joseph's bones were brought and buried.[1]
But a little distance southward,
Just a walk of but five minutes,
And they stood where Christ our Saviour,
With a love most condescending,
Leaning on the well of Jacob,
Spoke in mercy with that woman,
Who had come from near by Sychar,
To draw water fresh and sparkling.
Oh how strange were their sensations,
While at Jacob's well they lingered,
Reading from their Bagster's Bible
All about our Saviour's message
To the woman of Samaria.[2]
Musing o'er it thus wrote Edward :—

    See sitting there by Jacob's well,
        Beneath the noon-tide's ray,
    A stranger in that lovely dell,
        Draw near to Him, I pray.
    Oh! look within His lovely face,—
    You there Divinity can trace.

    Yes, yes, He is the Son of God,
        He came to earth from heaven;
    'Twas all to bear sin's awful load,
        That we might be forgiven—
    Our very nature now He wears,
    Our human sufferings He shares.

    But look! there comes from Sychar's gate
        A woman to that well;—

[1] Josh. xxiv. 32.   [2] John iv.

THE LIVING WATER.

The Lord of Glory to her spake,
   For He had much to tell.
He then, with wisdom most supreme,
Drew from her what her life had been.

She found her guilt by Him was known,
   Her sins, a black array,
Before His eye were clearly shown,
   As in the light of day.
No wonder she was much impressed
By Jesu's words, to her addressed.

If any man, He said, shall drink
   Of waters that I give,
Of thirst again he ne'er shall think;
   Within him there shall live
A fountain, pure, and sparkling bright,
As lovely as the morning light.

What wonder that the woman cried,
   ' Oh ! give me such I pray,
A fountain that shall ne'er be dried,—
   I 'll drink of it "for aye."'
He gave, she drank, **her thirst was gone**—
Then Jesu's love was **all her** song.

The water, which from Jacob's well
   She came with pot to bring,
She all forgot, and flew to tell,
   With joy that made her sing

Of One, who made her thirst indeed,
And then supplied her every need.

Then quickly they who heard her call
    Drew near to Jacob's well,
And there they saw the Lord of all,
    Who came to save from hell.
He preached, no doubt, to them the Word,
And many lived that day who heard.

But when the Lord's disciples saw
    The good results that day,
Then they were filled with sacred awe,
    And led in faith to pray,—
'Dear Saviour, make us more like Thee;
Help us to speak to all we see.

No matter tho' they are most vile,
    With sins too bad to name,
Altho' their hearts are full of guile,
    Their life but one of shame,
Still help us tell them of thy grace,
So free to all who seek Thy face.

'Tis true the harvest-fields are white—
    Not four months hence, but *now*.
Help us to work 'ere yet the night
    Sheds dew upon our brow,
That we may gather in the grain,
And thus for heaven some treasure gain.'

Up the sides of Mount Gerizim,[1]
By a path not often trodden,
Led by Jacobs, a Samaritan—
High Priest of the very order,
Who for centuries have worshipped
God upon that sacred mountain,
In accordance with their custom.

 From the top of that bold mountain,
On all sides the view was glorious.
Though 'twas in the month November,
Yet the air was soft and balmy,
Like a May-day in New England.

 They were pointed where a temple,
Or perhaps a Roman fortress,
Once was standing on Gerizim.

 Little cared they for the jargon
Of that priest so much deluded.

 In the world are not two hundred
Members of the church, Samaritan,
Yet their priest he talked about it,
As if they alone were righteous.

 While they lingered on that mountain,
They were often led to think of
Why 'twas called the mount of blessing.

 Long ago in days of Joshua,
All the people were assembled
In that lovely vale of Shechem,
Part upon the sides of Ebal,
To pronounce the dreaded curses
Of Jehovah against sinners;
While upon the Mount Gerizim,
There were seated those who uttered
Blessings rich upon God's chosen,
Who should always keep His precepts.

 But it was upon Mount Ebal,—
Yes, upon the mount of cursing,[2]

---

[1] Deut. xxvii. 12.   [2] Deut. xxvii. 13.

That the people all *rejoiced*¹—
For upon that mount was offered
Sacrifices, which then pointed
To the great atoning Saviour.
'*If*' was prefixed to each blessing.
Oh! how many now are climbing
Up some fancied Mount Gerizim,
Thinking they shall *merit* favour,
Ever seeking to get blessing,
By obeying laws most holy,
Yet no blessing comes unto them,
All because that it is written,
'All have sinned,' and all are guilty.
  But 'tis those, who face the *curses*,
And march boldly up Mount Ebal,
Thus acknowledging they're sinners,
And press forward to the altar,
Where the sacrifice is offered,
That atones for sin for ever.
  Blessed Jesus! He has said that
'Twas to call poor guilty '*sinners*,'
Who acknowledge their transgressions,—
Not the '*righteous*,' that He died for.
Jesus, in His walk so holy,
Climbed Gerizim, got the blessing,
Gathered all the flowers it beareth,
Brought them to the top of Ebal,—
There God's wrath was laid upon Him;—
There for you and me He suffered,—
All our sins were laid upon Him.
Oh! my reader, do you love Him?
Come, tho' guilty, He will save you,
For His sake God will forgive you.
Face the curses, make confession,
That you cannot climb Gerizim,
That *your* righteousness is useless,

¹ Deut. xxvii. 7.

That you cannot get the blessing,
All because the 'if' is with it;—
Yes, confess that you have broken
God's commandments and are guilty,
That your hope is all in Jesus,
Then like those upon Mount Ebal,
Filled your heart will be with singing,
Happy you will be for ever.

Riding south five hours from Shechem,
Through a country cultivated,
On their left there lay before them
Shiloh, now, alas! in ruins,
There it was the Tabernacle
Long remained with God's own presence;—
Thither came the little Samuel,
With his praying mother, Hannah,
To abide with good old Eli,
And before the Lord to worship,
Girded with a linen ephod.
On that hill-side there before them,
One night in the Holy Temple,
Little Samuel was awakened
By a voice he thought was Eli's:—
Quickly then he rose and hastened
To the bed-side of the High Priest,—
Saying, 'Here am I, thou call'd'st me.'[1]
But the answer he receivèd
Was, My son, lie down, I called not.
Thrice the call was then repeated,
Thrice the Lord called, Samuel, Samuel.
Thrice he rose, and ran to Eli
'Ere he saw 'twas God who called him,
Little thinking that Jehovah
Would stoop down to talk with Samuel.
When at last he this perceivèd,

[1] 1 Sam. iii. 3.

Then he told the child to answer,
'Speak, Lord, for Thy servant heareth.'
  Quickly then the child obeyèd,
And the Lord revealed to Samuel
Hidden secrets most important.
From that hour his God was with him,
And all knew he was a prophet,
Then he led a life most holy,
All because he listened early
To the call from God his Father.

  Oh! how many parents are there
Just like Eli in their blindness!
When the Lord speaks to their children,
They, alas! cannot believe it,
Thus for many years they linger,
Not believing that God calls them.

  Meanwhile Satan gets possession
Of the heart once young and tender,
Then, if e'er they are converted,
Terrible must be the struggle
On escaping from his fetters.

  Passing on thro' several places
Mentioned in the Sacred Scriptures,
As the golden sun was setting,
They approached a rugged hill-top,
Which was named by Jacob, Bethel;[1]
Surely there were stones sufficient
For the patriarchs and prophets,
Had they *all* with Jacob gathered,
And been searching each for pillows
Upon which to lay their heads down.

  As they strolled about by starlight,
On that 'place' where Jacob's ladder
Reached from earth up to the heaven,—
Then they thought much of the promise
Made by God unto His servants,

[1] Gen. xxviii. 19.

When the angels were ascending
And descending on the ladder,[1]
  'I the God am of thy Fathers,
God of Abraham and Isaac,
I am with thee and will keep thee
In the places where thou goest,
To this land again I'll bring thee.'
  Then they prayed that God *their* Father
Might go with them, as with Jacob,
That they might with him be saying,
'This most surely is the house of
God, and 'tis the gate of heaven.'
  Then they thought of how the name of
Bethel, 'house of God,' was changed to
Beth-a-ven—the 'house of idols,'
And they asked that their own hearts might
Ever truly be called 'Bethels;'—
That they might be temples fitted
For the Spirit's constant dwelling,
Where the blessed Saviour's presence
Ever should be felt and cherished.[2]
  While they saw the stars of heaven,
All so quiet, gazing on them,
The same stars that looked on Jacob,
Then they felt *their* Father likewise,
Was the same who watched o'er Jacob,
And that He was just as ready
To watch o'er them as o'er Jacob.
  Bethel now is come to nothing,[3]
As foretold by Prophet Amos,
Only a few wretched people
Linger where were the assemblies,
In the days when once the judges
Were the rulers of the people,
And where once King Jeroboam,
As he stood beside the altar,

[1] Gen. xxviii. 13-15. [2] John xiv. 21. [3] Amos v. 5.

Filled with anger at the prophet
For his words of solemn warning,
Found his hand so quickly withered
When he made th' attempt to stop him.[1]

While they tarried there at Bethel,
Oft they thought of good Elisha,
And of how the Bethel children
Mocked him, crying, 'Go, thou bald-head,'
And of how the hungry bears
Tore in pieces over forty,
For their wickedness so glaring.

'Twas from Bethel, with their glasses,
They first saw the Holy City,
Shining in the morning sun-light,
Tho' it was some twelve miles distant.

On their left they passed by Ai,[2]
The most ancient of the cities
In the land of Palestina,
Celebrated for its capture,[3]
After Jericho had fallen;
Also they passed right thro' Beeroth,
One of those four crafty cities,
Who, with tale so melancholy,
Misled Joshua at Gilgal,
Till he promised he would never
War against them in their country.
To the right stood Neby Samuel,
Which now marks the site of Ramah,
Where was born the Prophet Samuel,
And there also once stood Mizpeh,
Where was raised the stone memorial,
With the name of Ebenezer—
'Hitherto the Lord hath helped us,'[4]

There at Mizpeh Saul was chosen
To be king o'er all of Israel.
There it was too, that King Richard,

[1] 1 Kings xiii.   [2] Gen. xii. 8.   [3] Josh. viii.   [4] 1 Sam. vii.

He oft called the lion-hearted,
Having left his camp at Ajalon,
As Jerusalem burst on him,
Cried, 'Lord God, oh! let me never
Walk within the Holy City,
If I may not it recapture
From the hands of all its enemies.'
  On their right was also Gibeon,
Where was murdered David's nephew
By his crafty cousin Joab,[1]
Where, too, Solomon once offered
To the Lord a thousand offerings,
And where God appeared unto him,
Promising that He would give him
Understanding and great wisdom,
Riches also, and much honour,[2]
While approaching to the city,
They drew near a rounded hill-top,
Which in days of Saul was Gibeah.[3]
To the top of it rode Edward,
Not another one was with him;—
Much resembled it Samaria
On all sides the view was glorious;
Wise was Saul in having chosen
It as his own royal residence.

[1] 2 Sam. xx.   [2] 1 Kings iii. 9-15.   [3] 1 Sam. xxiii. 19.

CHAPTER XV.

'TWAS the first day of December,
And the air was soft and balmy,
As in days of 'Indian Summer,'
When ascended on Mount Scopus,
Burst upon them, in full glory,
Zion and the Holy City.

Plain they saw the Mosque of Omar,
Built where once the ancient Temple,
Rose in majesty and glory;—
Saw the church built o'er the sepulchre,
Where, 'tis said, our Lord once rested.

Every hat at once was lifted,
As they stood upon that hill-top.

Surely then it was no wonder
That their eyes were filled with tears,
When they clearly saw that city
In which Christ our Lord once suffered
For a guilty world's redemption.

Not a breath of air was moving,
Not a sound disturbed their musing,
Oh! how solemn and impressive
Was their first full view of Zion,
And Mount Olives in the distance!

As they near approached the city,
First its wall so very lofty,
Then attracted their attention.

Passing by the gate Damascus,
On the western side they entered,

Through the gate, by which from Joppa,
All find entrance to the city.
 On their right the 'Tower of David,'
Solid, massive, rose before them.
 First their steps were to their bankers,
Where were numerous letters for them,
From their friends across the water.
 Hard it was for them to realize,
They were in the Holy City,
Reading letters from their kindred,
Many thousand furlongs distant.
 Full of gratitude their hearts were,
For the news they found so cheering
From their parents and their loved ones.
 Oh! how could they but be thankful
To the God of all their mercies,
That they had escaped the dangers
Of their long and perilous journey.
 After having read their letters,
The first place they sought to visit,
Was the spot where Christ was offered,
That He might atone for sinners:—
Therefore, ere the shades of evening
Closed around them, they were standing
On the spot where, says tradition,
Jesus Christ was once uplifted
On the cross, for sinners ruined,
Who the laws of God had broken.
 Well they knew it was disputed,—
Yet the fact that thousands go there,
To the Church of Holy Sepulchre,
Filled with awe and solemn rev'rence,
Led them also each to view it
With the deepest kind of interest.
 'Tis a grand and gorgeous building,
Built by the Empress Helena,
In about the year three hundred.

Near the door-way, as they entered,
Was a slab of finest marble,
Upon which, 'tis said, our Saviour
Was laid down to be anointed,
When He from the cross was taken.

But a little farther left-ward,
They were taken to the sepulchre,
In which they were told the body
Of our Lord three days reposèd,
And from which He rose triumphant,
Over death and hell victorious.

'Tis a low room, six by seven,
With its stones worn smooth by kisses
Of the pilgrims from all nations.
It was full when they approached it,
But 'twas soon their turn to enter.
There they saw the lamps all golden,
Which by day and night are burning,
Forty-two, no less in number,—
Surely it was most impressive,
There to see the awe-struck pilgrims
Sobbing till their hearts seemed breaking,
While they kissed the stones before them.

Soon they found their way to Calvary,
Where for nearly fifteen centuries,
Since the days of good Eusebius,
Thousands, thousands have regarded
As the very spot upon which
Christ was offered up a ransom.

Formerly the place was covered
With a building, separated
From the one built o'er the sepulchre:
But the Church is now extended,
So that both the sacred places
Now are underneath one covering.

There a boy of but eight summers,

Near the spot where by his father,
He was taught Christ died for children,
On the stones was kneeling, praying.
  How they wished they knew his language,
That they more of Christ might tell him,
Of his cruel death and sufferings,
And of how He now is waiting
To receive all little children,
Who will only come and trust Him.
Yet they offered the petition,
That he by the Spirit's teaching
Might be led to trust in Jesus,
And be fitted thus for heaven.
  They of one thing felt quite certain,
That not far from where they then were,
Jesus for their sins once suffered.
These were thoughts that Edward Payson
Had while standing near Golgotha : —

    Here it was the Lord of Glory
      At Golgotha died for me,
    Here I read the wond'rous story
      Of His death to set me free.

    Here His hands and feet all bleeding,
      Fast were nailed unto the cross ;
    Here His wounds for me were pleading,
      When my gain was all His loss.

    Here by God He was forsaken,
      When He took the sinner's place,
    For his sake I now am taken
      Into favour under grace.

Here the sword of justice slew Him,
  That I might be justified;
Praise the Lord I ever knew Him,
  That for me He bled and died.

Blessed Jesus, I will love Thee,
  Love Thee till my latest breath,
And in Heaven I will adore Thee,
  When these eyes are closed in death.

  Much within the Holy Sepulchre,
Every day they saw of interest.
  There were Greeks from far-off Russia
Singing hymns by St. Chrysostom,
Which so long ago were chanted
On the lonely shores of Bosphorus.
  There they saw th' ambitious Latins,
To the Pope far more devoted
Than to Jesus Christ our Saviour.
  There also were the Armenians,
From the bottom of that mountain
On which once the Ark of wood was
Resting after all its wanderings
O'er the dreary waste of waters,—
There were Maronites from Lebanon,
And the Copts from Lower Egypt;
Then they thought of that bless'd Pentecost,
When from 'out of every nation,'
There were 'dwelling at Jerusalem,'
Men devout yet unconverted.
Oh! how much they longed to see there
Such another day of Pentecost,
And some Peter boldly speaking,
Boldly preaching to them Jesus,

As the risen Lord of Glory,
Who will surely judge the nations
On that day by God appointed.
   Every day while in the city,
They were vis'tors to the Sepulchre.
Many go there just to speculate,
And to show their wondrous learning,
In disputing what tradition
Has affirmed for fifteen centuries.
   If one spot above another
Must be held by all as sacred,
Sure 'twould be where Christ was offered
Up a sacrifice for sinners.
Even granting no one knows where
Christ our Lord became our Surety,
Still the fact that thousand thousands
Have for eighteen hundred years
Knelt beside the rock that's riven,
And with many tears bedewed it,
Firm believing that our Saviour
There upon the cross was wounded,
Is enough to make it sacred,
And to cause all who approach it
To be filled with deepest reverence.
Thousands thousands now in glory,
Who were pious men and humble,
Have, with hearts and brows all throbbing,
Knelt and prayed and sanctified it.
   Travellers in Eastern countries
Oft of mummery get tired,
Yet who can but deeply sympathize
With the pilgrims from all nations,
Who may love to come and worship
At the spot where Jesus suffered,
And where He three days was buried?
Call it, if you will, idolatry—

Bigotry, e'en some would term it,
Yet, perchance, there very many
Think of Jesus' death on Calvary,
And while praying learn to trust Him.
 Even in the Holy Sepulchre,
Though possessed of many errors
In their creeds and in their doctrines,
Yet perhaps the death of Jesus
Is made to them a reality,
So that they there learn to love Him,
By their visits to the places
Where He bore the guilt of sinners,
And where o'er grim death He triumphed,
Bursting there its bonds asunder.

 Mount of Olives! O what memories
Cluster round the very mention
Of that name, to us so sacred!
 After having on Mount Zion
Broken bread with Christ's disciples—
No great distance from the place where
Our Lord's Supper first was eaten—
Then the pilgrims from America
'Went unto the Mount of Olives,'
There to read the Holy Bible,
And to call to mind more fully
Sacred scenes thereon enacted.
 Down into the Vale of Kedron
They went by the very pathway
Which our Saviour often traversed
On His way to that retirement,
Which He sought for on the hill-side,
When of yore 'twas thickly covered
With the olive trees so lovely.
 Oh! how glorious was the prospect
From the mount where Jesus sometimes

Spent the night in earnest pleadings.[1]
  Near the Church of the Ascension
Was their finest panorama
Of Jerusalem, 'the Holy.'
Nearest to them—Mosque of Omar,
Covering all of Mount Moriah.
  Farther on, the Armenian Convent
Rose majestic on Mount Zion.
  To the right the Holy Sepulchre
Was a most conspicuous object.
  Turning to the east they saw then,
Far across the Jordan's valley,
Moab's mountains, steep and rugged;
And 'twas there they first were favoured
With a sight of those dread waters,
Which now flow where once Gomorrah,
And where Sodom stood—proud cities.
  But while on the Mount of Olives,
They much oftener thought of Jesus,
And of how upon that mountain
Oft He sat with His disciples,
Telling them of the destruction
Of Jerusalem before them,—
Also of the persecutions,
Which most surely should befal them,
Ere their last and final triumph.
  There it was, too, they remembered
That our Lord from earth ascended,[2]
Having said to His disciples,
'Go ye forth and preach the Gospel
To the world, to *every creature;*
Go, and I will e'er be with you.[3]
Also, power shall be granted,
If ye will wait for the promise
To you given by the Father.'

---

[1] Luke vi. 12.   [2] Acts i. 1, 2.   [3] Matt. xxviii. 19, 20; Acts i. 8.

There it was, while they stood gazing,
Looking steadfastly toward heaven,
That two men in white apparel,
With angelic mien and bearing,
'Stood by them,' and told them Jesus
Should return in the like manner
As they'd seen Him enter heaven.

May God grant that when He cometh[1]
We may each be ready waiting,
And be found among the number
Who shall 'look for His appearing.'[2]

Down the mountain slow they wandered,
To the town where once lived Mary,
With her brother and with Martha;
When our Saviour oft was wearied
With His labours in the city,
There He rested, filled with longings
For that deep and heartfelt sympathy,
Which He knew for Him was waiting
'Neath the roof of those dear loved ones.

They were first led to the ruins
Of the house of him whom Jesus
Raised from dust, tho' he'd been sleeping
In the grave four days together.

There they knew the loving sisters
Oft had run to meet their Master
When they saw Him coming to them.
From their house no doubt they often
Came to look away toward Jericho,
When their brother fast was sinking,
Yea, and when he then was dying.

Gathering there some leaves and flowers,
Then they turnèd to that spot where
Long tradition says that Lazarus
In the grave four days lay sleeping.

Vividly then came before them

[1] Matt. xxv. 1.   [2] Heb. ix. 28.

The events of that last miracle
Which the loving heart of Jesus
Prompted Him to work in Bethany.
   There they seemed to see Him weeping[1]
Who, for reasons full of wisdom,
Had for days delayed His coming.
Then it was they heard Him saying,
' Let the stone away be taken,'
Then His voice, which reached to heaven,
Summoned from the dead the brother.
   There stood Martha, pale and trembling,
And the loving Mary, gazing
At the form which from death started,
When the mighty word of Jesus
First disturbed the solemn silence
In the 'cave,' where it was resting.
   When they saw 'twas really Lazarus,
With what joy, that's past expressing,
Did they clasp him to their bosoms,
Printing on his lips fond kisses,
Asking questions—Oh! how eager!
   Most impressive 'twas to stand there,
Right in Bethany, and witness
That bless'd scene, in which our Saviour's
Loving heart was all disclosèd.
   Then they heard their Master saying,
' I am Life and Resurrection;
He that upon me believeth,
He may die, but yet he liveth.'[2]
   Before leaving they descended
To the cave, in which tradition
Says that Lazarus was buried.
Twice ten feet below the surface,
There they found a room, sepulchral,
Where no doubt some one was buried,
And why not believe 'twas Lazarus?

[1] John xi. 35.   [2] John xi.

On returning to Jerusalem,
They went by a different pathway
Than the one which they had taken
When they came from it to Bethany.
In the steps of Christ they followed,
On the day of His triumphal
Entrance to the Holy City,
Keeping near the foot of Olivet;
And they also clearly saw where
Jesus once wept o'er the city,[1]
On account of its not knowing
Of its day of visitation.

Then they felt, alas! how little
They possessed of Christ's compassion
For the guilty and the dying!
And they prayed that He would give them
Greater tenderness for sinners,
So that when they spake of danger,
They might do so in a manner
That should win all hearts the rather
Than that they by it be hardened.

They will ne'er forget the feelings,
Which they had when first the city
Burst upon them as they rounded
A projecting spur of Olivet;
Here, they said, the feet of Jesus
Stood when down His cheeks the tears
Spoke of His great heart of pity
For the city which rejected
All His warnings and entreaties.

The Son of God o'er sinners weeps,
  Because they will not hear His cry!
How hard the heart must be that keeps
  Its love from Him who came to die!

[1] Luke xix. 41.

Oh! Jesus, make us more like Thee,
    That we may warn, but yet with tears;
And then from wrath will sinners flee,
    And Thou wilt shield them from their fears.

Oh! draw us nearer to Thy heart,
    That we may feel its throbs of love;
Then when we preach, the tears will start,
    And all will seek a home above.

Oh! sinners, think of Him who shed
    For you His tears of heartfelt grief.
Oh! come and trust in Him who bled,
    That you from sin might find relief.

CHAPTER XVI.

MOSQUE of Omar claims attention,
  For 'twas on its site the Temple
  Stood in majesty and glory.
Therefore thither went the party,
After having made arrangements
With the Sheik for their admission,
On receiving one pound sterling.
  Only recently have travellers
Been admitted by the Moslems
To the place to them so sacred.
  Bright the sun was shining on them
When they stood on Mount Moriah,
Where once Abraham, with Isaac,
Came to make of him an offering.
  Then the 'slippers' from Damascus
Were found useful for this visit,
For they found that none could enter
With the shoes that they'd been wearing.
  As they passed along the pavement,
Which for years, almost six hundred,
Had alone been trod by Moslems,
They observed that it was largely
Of Moriah's rock, all polished,
When by Solomon 'twas levelled [1]
By his 'hewers' and 'stone squarers.'
  O'er that pavement had walked Jesus,
When a child of but twelve summers,

[1] 1 Kings v.

And in later years when burdened
With the thoughts of His high mission,
That same pavement had been sprinkled
With the blood of Jews defending
Their loved temple from the Romans.
   There the Saracens and Christians
Long had fought till by death conquered.
   There it was that the great Saladin
Sprinkled it with sweet rose-water,
Thus to cleanse it from pollution.
   They at length amazed were standing
On the Mosque built where Araunah
Had his level floor for threshing,[1]
And where David built an altar.[2]
   Oh! how gorgeous was that building,
With its dome all full of rainbows,
Braided into one bright tissue.
At the base around all lighted
With a rainbow which seemed brighter
And more splendid than the others.
When a thousand lamps are burning
'Neath this dome, oh! how resplendent
Then appears the Mosque of Omar.
   But to Ida, and to Edward,
The great rock was more attractive,
Which the Mosque seems built to honour.
'Twas the top of old Moriah;
'Twas the altar of burnt offering,[3]
Where, when Solomon was praying,
Fire came down from out of heaven.[4]
Toward that rock all Israel worshipped,
Sixty feet in length it measures,
While in width it is near forty,
And in height in feet near seventeen,
Showing that to build the temple,

---

[1] 2 Sam. xxiv.   [2] 2 Sam. xxiv. 25.   [3] 1 Chron. xxii. 1.
                        [4] 2 Chron. vii. 1.

Solomon cut away the hill-top;
Thus the rock was left projecting,
Even in the holy temple.
  In the year about nine hundred,
When the Moslem Omar found it,
Then 'twas covered o'er with rubbish.
  There he built a Mosque far fairer
Than his other fourteen hundred.
  Underneath it went the pilgrims,
Where they found a little chamber
Where the Moslems pray to Allah.
  There they saw some broken pillars,
Which were once built in the temple.
  They were told that from that cavity
Led a passage to the place where
Once were treasures of the temple.
  Then away to Mosque-el-Aksa,—
It was once a church for Christians,
Built by Emperor Justinian;
Now 'tis used to worship Allah.
'Tis a large and massive structure,
With gigantic, solid columns.
Underneath the Mosque-el-Aksa
Are the ancient crypts so famous.
There they saw the great foundations
Which were once in Solomon's temple,
There were stones in size enormous,
Eight by fifteen feet they measured.—
Once more 'neath the light of heaven
They were standing by the golden
Porch of Solomon, called the 'Beautiful.'[1]
  Still it stands as in the days when
John and Peter through it entered
On their way into the temple.
  There it was they found the lame man
Asking alms of all who passed him,

[1] Acts iii. 1, 2.

But as Peter had no silver,
He did that which was far better,—
For 'twas through the name of Jesus,
That he from his lameness healed him,—
So that he was soon found walking,
Praising God within the temple.

   Like some ancient massive building,
Is the gate that's still called Golden.
The stone roof is well supported
By six lofty dome-shaped arches,
On some polished marble columns.
   Now 'tis called the tomb of Solomon,
By tradition not well founded.
   Many thoughts oft pressed upon them
While they wandered o'er Moriah.
   Like a vision passed before them
Abraham, Isaac, David, Solomon,
Jotham, Ahaz, Hezekiah,
Nahum, Micah, Jeremiah;
But they oftener thought of Jesus,—
How He trod upon that pavement,
How He there once preached the Gospel,
How at Feast of Tabernacles,
At that last great day, the Saviour
Stood and said, 'Whoso that thirsteth,
Let him drink the living water
Which I give to all who seek it,
Then his words shall water others.'[1]

   Passing from that vast arena,
Which belonged once to the temple,—
Soon the pilgrims reached Bethesda:—
There, their guide told them tradition
Fixed the place where once the Saviour
Healed the man from childhood smitten,
Who for years, full eight and thirty,

[1] John vii. 37.

Had with a disease been suffering,
Long had waited for assistance,
When the waters oft were troubled,
But the others were before him.
 There it was, at least they say so,
That the loving Jesus told him,
' Rise, take up thy bed,' and quickly
Rose the man and praised his Maker.
The remains of the five porches
They discovered (or they thought so)
In which once lay a great number
Of the blind and halt all waiting
For the moving of the waters.
 Then they thought, alas! how often
At the pool of ordinances
Sinners long impatient linger,
When beside them their Redeemer
Stands with mighty power from heaven,
Full of tender, loving kindness,
Able, willing, in a moment,
To recover them completely,
And to make them fit for glory.
Have you turned to Him, my reader?
Near you He is standing, waiting,
See His side for you once wounded,
Whence there flowed a wondrous fountain,
In its power, more efficacious,
Than was e'er the Pool Bethesda.
 Yes, 'tis He who died for sinners,
Shed His life-blood for the guilty,
And who opened up a fountain [1]
For all sin and for uncleanness.
Yes, His blood from all sin cleanseth.[2]
Then they asked to see where Pilate
Dwelt when he condemned our Saviour
To the death of crucifixion.

[1] Zech. xiii. 1.   [2] 1 John i. 7.

They were shown where once the steps were
Which led down from the Prætorium,
In which Christ was scourged and beaten.
Once those steps by Christ were trodden,
Now the Latins say they have them
In the church they call St. Lataran.
When in Rome they saw all ages,
On their knees with heavy burdens,
Going up them often praying,
Trusting in this act of penance
Rather than in Christ the Saviour,
Who for them the work has ' finished.'
Long the strangers from America
Lingered round the spot where Jesus
For our sakes was sorely wounded.
  Then they turned their steps towards Calvary,
Through the Via Dolorosa,
Where 'tis said our Saviour bore the
Cross for us to Calvary's mountains.
  First they came to Ecce Homo,
'Tis a strange and quaint old archway,
Which perhaps stood there when Pilate
Sought to have them free our Saviour
Rather than the vile Barabbas.
  On their way a little farther,
They were pointed to the place where
Jesus fell with pain, exhausted,
Fell beneath the cross so heavy,—
And the house of Veronica,
Who when Christ was passing by it,
Moved with pity and compassion,
Came and handed Him the kerchief,
That the bloody perspiration
From His brow might then be taken.
  There are now some fifteen stations,
Where oft pray the weary pilgrims,

From the house of guilty Pilate,
To the place once called Golgotha,
Each one marked with name of Jesus,
All connected with some incident
Of that journey to Mount Calvary.
Tho' no doubt they are fictitious,
Still that heart must be most hardened,
That can walk that way unmoved.
In the notes of Edward Payson
Are these jottings which we give you :—

    In Pilate's house behold
        The blessed Saviour bound;
    His marble brow all deathly cold,
        With thorns He there is crowned.

    Draw near to Him, I pray,
        He's wounded there for thee;
    Oh! do not turn from Him away,
        List to that mockery.

    Oh! see those cruel stripes
        Upon His back all bare,
    See from His bleeding brow He wipes
        The blood that trickles there.

    That blood was shed for thee,
        For thee 'twas freely spilt,
    From all thy sins to set thee free,
        And cleanse away thy guilt.

He died that thou mightst live,
    Oh ! come and trust Him now,
He'll freely all thy sins forgive,
    And clothe with **peace** thy brow.

Now say—O Lord !—I pray,
    For Jesus' sake **alone,**
Take all my guilt and sins away,
    And make me all thine own.

CHAPTER XVII.

WHEN their friends in dear New England,
And upon the Susquehanna,
With the biting cold were shivering
In the middle of December,
Then 'twas Edward and his Ida,
With their constant friends from Brooklyn,
Started for the vale of Jordan.
   Long before them went the servants,
With the tents, and with the baggage,
To make ready for their coming.
   Fresh and eager were their horses,
For the journey 'down to Jericho.'
   Their first station was to Bethany,
To the place where Christ so often
Came all weary from the city,
Where He knew that Martha, Mary,
Would be ready to receive Him.
Gathering flowers for their herbarium,
From beside the tomb of Lazarus,
As they passed by the same road which
Jesus once came up from Jericho,
On His way to crucifixion.
Every rock and stone seemed hallowed,
For they each had seen our Saviour
On His way to raise up Lazarus,
From the tomb where he lay sleeping.
Yes, and they had looked upon Him,

When His loving heart was burning
With compassion for lost sinners,
Leading Him to go straight forward,
When He knew that He must suffer
More than mortals e'er can think of,—
Not mere tortures of the body,
But, alas! something more dreadful
Than the crown and cruel scourging,
Than the cross with all its horrors,
With its mockings and revilings;
Yea, alas! when He was sure that
As He took the place of sinners,
God must turn in justice from Him,
And that He in deepest sorrow
Would cry out with tears and anguish,
'Why, O God!—am I forsaken?'
Thus, dear Jesus! we would see Thee,
When we think of all Thy sufferings
For our guilty souls endurèd.

    After sev'ral miles of travel,
They approached the place tradition
Says was where the good Samaritan
Brought the man who had been wounded
'To an inn,' where he was cared for.[1]

    Having watered there their horses,
On their rugged way they hastened.

    On their left lay Quarantonia,
That 'high mountain,' where our **Saviour**
Long was tempted by the devil,
Who by Him was each time baffled
With quotations from the Bible,[2]
Always saying, 'It is written.'

    There the sight of that bold mountain
Drew their hearts more close to Jesus,
Leading them to think how He was

[1] Luke x. 34. [2] Matt. iv.

In all points like them oft tempted,
Yet without once ever yielding.
  Then they prayed that He, who conquered
All the mighty powers of darkness,
Would sustain them in their trials,
Make them strong to fight the devil,
Knowing well his arch devices.
  Before passing to the valley,
Their way led them where Elijah
Long ago was fed by ravens,
While upon the banks of Cherith.
  Oft they seemed to hear their Father,
He who once sustained Elijah,
' If thou wilt but only trust me,
I will never, never leave thee,
I will feed thee and will clothe thee,
I will keep thee, I will bless thee,
I will be to thee a Father.'
  Thus encouraged on they galloped,
To the place where once the city
Of the 'Palm Trees' long was stationed.
Their imagination pictured
Jericho six days besiegèd
By the mighty hosts of Joshua,
On all sides by them encompassed,
While above the rest there sounded
Clear a voice,[1] ' Shout—for the city
Now the Lord to you has given.'
Then the lofty walls were shaken,
Yea, and to the earth fell prostrate.
  Then they felt that God was mighty,
That if they would only trust Him,
Using also means appointed,
That in many, many cities,
Walls of sin and vice and folly
Would, when sounds the gospel trumpet,

        [1] Joshua vi. 16.

Then be shaken and would totter,
Thus permitting truth to enter,
And to conquer all the people,
Leading them to sweet submission
To their Lord, their rightful master.

 To the east of where stood Jericho,
Was a poor and wretched hamlet,
There they found their tents and servants.
They were glad enough to see them,
And were ready for their dinner,
Which was smoking hot and waiting.

 Near them flowed some of the water,
Flowing from Elisha's fountain,[1]
Which by him was changed to sweetness:—
Glad enough were they to drink it.

 Then they thought of how important
That the heart in early childhood
Should be cleansed, that it might send both
Thoughts and words as pure as water
Bubbling from Elisha's fountain.

 As they gazed where once the 'city'
Of the palm trees rose in beauty,
Oft they thought of how Zaccheus
Climbed a tree to see the Saviour,
Little thinking Christ would call him,
And that day his house would enter
To partake of hospitality,
And to grant to him salvation.[2]

 Oft they seemed to hear Bartimeus
Crying, 'Jesus, Son of David,
Now I *pray have mercy on me.*'
Well he knew the crowd was passing,
That the Saviour was attended
By a num'rous band of people,
Anxious each to pay Him homage,
And that he himself was begging,

[1] 2 Kings ii. 17-20.   [2] Luke xix. 1.

Yes, a blind and wretched beggar,
Yet he knew that Christ was gracious,
And no doubt he oft had listened
To the story of His healing
A poor creature born with blindness;
So altho' the people bade him
Hold his peace and keep in silence,
Yet he only cried the louder,
'Son of David, oh! have mercy'—
Ah! but will the Saviour tarry?
Will He stop the crowd to listen
To the prayers of a blind beggar?

To Jerusalem He's hastening
To accomplish the redemption
Of a world that's lost and ruined.
Can He turn from His great mission
To have mercy on a blind man—
A poor pauper by the wayside?
Yes, oh! yes, He has compassion,
See! he stands beside the blind man,
Asking him for his petition.
Quickly then his prayer He answered,
Straightway He his sight received,
And his praises swelled the chorus
Of the anthem hallelujah.

Had he not then cried for mercy,
He would ne'er have seen the Saviour.

Reader, you were born in blindness,
Blind to sin and its destruction,
Blind to Christ and His salvation,
Blind to holiness and heaven.

Have you cried, 'Have mercy on me?'
Jesus' heart is still as tender
As when He once healed the blind man.
Yes, and He is now as mighty,
'Look to Him,' and you will *see* Him;

For He then your eyes will open,
If you look to Him for mercy,
Saying, 'Give me sight, I pray Thee.'
    Finally, they turned their faces
To the rugged banks of Jordan.
All in vain they looked for Gilgal,
Where was Israel's first encampment
On the eastern side of Jordan,[1]
Where they set the tabernacle,
Till it found a place in Shiloh.[2]
    In an hour the numerous party
Stood beside the 'Swift Descender'—
Worthy name for such a river,
Flowing onward with such swiftness,
From the base of snowy Lebanon
To the sea, so dark and gloomy,
Fringed its banks with oleander,
Tamarisk, and drooping willows;
Not a little like the Tiber
Then appeared the River Jordan.
    Tho' it was in truth ice water,
Still they followed the example
Of the multitudes, who bathe in
Jordan's waters, held so sacred.
Edward once was 'neath the surface
Of the turbid, rapid river,
Tho' the day was mild as summer,
Icy cold was Jordan's water.
    Having from it filled their bottles,
Still they lingered on its borders,
Thinking of the time 'twas parted
For the mighty hosts of Israel,
That they might pass on in safety[3]
To the land of milk and honey,—
To the land to them long promised,—

[1] Josh. iv.   [2] Josh. xviii.   [3] Josh. iii.

Even when they were in Egypt,—
Yea, to Jacob when in Bethel.
  There they seemed to see Elijah
Passing over in a pathway,
Safe and dry right thro' the waters.
On the other side they saw him,
Passing to the clouds of heaven
In a chariot all of fire,
Drawn by fiery horses also,
While upon the good Elisha
Fell the mantle of Elijah,
With which he too stood by Jordan,
And with which he smote its waters,
Till they parted 'hither, thither,'
For the prophet to pass over.
But the scene which most they thought of
Was that one of thrilling interest—
THE BAPTISM OF OUR SAVIOUR,
Which, according to tradition,
Once took place near where they halted;
When the Holy Spirit rested
Like a dove, lighting upon Him,
And when lo! a voice from heaven
Said, 'This is My Son Beloved.'[1]
  When they saw where oft 'the swellings'
Fill its banks to overflowing,
Then of death they oft were thinking,
Of the river on the border
Of our promised heavenly Canaan.
Then they each one joined in singing:—

  'Sweet fields beyond the swelling flood
    Stand dressed in living green;
  So to the Jews old Canaan stood,
    While Jordan rolled between.

[1] Matt. iii.

> But tim'rous mortals start and shrink,
>   To cross this narrow sea;
> And linger, shivering on the brink,
>   And fear to launch away.
>
> Oh! could we make our doubts remove—
>   Those gloomy doubts that rise,
> And view the Canaan that we love
>   With unbeclouded eyes.
>
> Could we but climb where Moses stood,
>   And view the landscape o'er,
> Not Jordan's stream, nor death's cold flood,
>   Should fright us from the shore.'

Ah! how could they then but offer
Up the prayer that God would help them
When at last they reach death's river,
That their Saviour then might bear them
Up amid the swelling Jordan;
That His rod and staff might comfort,
So that they should fear no evil,
But at last be safely landed
On the shore so bright and shining,
Ever feeling that beneath them
Are the mighty arms of Jesus.

   To the south they turned their faces,
Toward the place where once stood Sodom
And Gomorrah—Ah! how wicked!—
Now their very site is covered
With the Dead Sea's bitter waters.
   Having reached them, they proceeded

Each to try his skill in bathing.
A brisk wind rolled high its breakers
On the beach so smooth and sandy,
So that o'er them dashed the waters,
Some of which went 'neath their eyelids,
Pricking them like many needles,
Filling them with bitter anguish.
  On his back one of the party
Sought to read within his Bible,
But the heavy swelling water
Quickly turned him, rolled him over,
And beneath the briny surface
Went his Bible, wet entirely.
Edward also, most unwisely,
Tried while lying on the water
First to see if he could read from
The '*American Presbyterian*,'
Like the doctor, *he rolled over*,—
Filled his eyes with bitter water,—
Spoiled the paper he was reading.
When their eyes had once done aching,
Loud they laughed at their endeavour.
  Having dressed themselves, they found that
They seemed still wet with the waters
In which they had just been bathing.
Saturated was their clothing,
Unaffected by the sunshine.
Oh! how long they were in drying!
  Meditating on the Jordan,
And of how they now had followed
It in all its devious wanderings,
From its birth to its last resting,
It seemed like some human being.
Thinking of it while on horseback,
Edward jotted in his note-book
Lines perchance to you of interest:—

LINES ON THE JORDAN.

I stood beside the bubbling spring
   From which the Jordan has its birth,
And seemed to hear its waters sing,
   As they come sparkling from the earth,—
'We from our prison-house are free,
The beauteous world we now shall see.'

Like reckless youth they dashed along,
   Coquetting with the flowers so fair,
And oft I seemed to hear their song,
   As they went laughing everywhere,—
'We o'er the earth may roam at will,
In every place be merry still.'

One day as they went singing by,
   Kissing each flower that bowed its head,
The golden sun from out the sky,
   Then to the youthful river said,—
'Wouldst thou in very truth be free?
Then one day thou shalt dwell with me.'

At length its chafing waters dwelt
   Within the Sea of Galilee;—
Restraints of youth no longer felt,
   I seemed to hear it say to me,—
'Here shall my manhood's days be passed,
For hitherto we've run too fast.'

But one day near the southern shore,
   The waters born at Jordan's spring

Within the lake were seen no more,
    And pensively I heard them sing,—
'That joyous lake we now have left;
    We're hastening to the sea of death.'

The waters, trembling, rolled along,
    Down, down toward the bitter sea,
Anon I heard their mournful song
    While borne away from Galilee,—
'And must we then forgotten be,
In yonder sea for ever die?'

Thus filled with many doubts and fears,
    The waters of the Jordan fell
Into that sea filled with the tears
    Of Sodom sinners lost in hell:—
The glorious sun with kindly power,
    Was with them in their dying hour.

The promise which when in their youth,
    They from the shining sun had heard,
Was then vouchsafed in very truth,
    And yet again they heard his word,—
'All pure—you now shall dwell with me,
    Yon beauteous sky your home shall be.'

Oh! Jordan, I would ever mind
    The lesson thou hast taught to me,
And when I near the verge of time,
    From doubts and fears may I be free—

Oh! Sun of Righteousness Divine,
   Then take me to that home of Thine.

With triumph then I can exclaim,
   Grim death to me it has no sting,
To all around I will proclaim,
   Thanks be to God, He makes me sing,—
'The sting of death is only sin,
   Thro' Christ the victory we win.'

   Ne'er will Edward and Eliza,
Nor the friends who journeyed with them,
Soon forget the solemn thoughts that
Pressed upon them while they gazed on
Those dark waters thirteen hundred
Feet below the Mediterranean,
Stretching forty miles to southward,
Yet ne'er finding any outlet.
   They were carried back four thousand
Years ago when Abraham's nephew
Looked toward Sodom from a mountain,
And beheld the plain of Jordan
Watered well and most attractive.[1]
   But he thought, alas! too little,
Of the sinful men who dwelt there.
   Little knew he of the vengeance
Which would one day fall upon them,
For their sins against high heaven.
   As the party climbed the mountain,
Overlooking all those waters,
Even to the south where Sodom
And Gomorrah once were stationed,
   Then they seemed to see those cities
On the borders of the Lakelet,

[1] Gen. xiii. 10.

All unconscious of their danger,
Even tho' their sins had risen
Up to heaven, and were calling
Down upon them direful vengeance.

On some mountain there before them,
'Twas that Abram long had pleaded
With the Lord for wicked Sodom,
That if there were fifty righteous,
For their sake He'd save those cities.

There it was he got the promise,
That if only ten were found there,
Who in very truth were righteous,
For their sakes God would have mercy.

But alas! not half that number
Righteous people dwelt within it,—
Therefore at the hour of even
Came two angels down to Sodom,
Came as messengers from Heaven,
To foretell the dire destruction
Which awaited all who tarried
In the cities doomed by heaven.

Even Lot they found half sleeping,
Even he would fain have lingered,
Till destruction overtook him—
Yet his warnings to his children
Seemed to them a madman's ravings,
Or like one who sure was mocking.[1]

Thus, alas! 'tis oft that sinners
In the city of destruction,
Told most plainly of their danger,
Only scoff at those who warn them,
Call them crazy or deluded.
But, alas! when the Lord Jesus
Cometh with His mighty angels,
Taking vengeance on the wicked,
Pouring on them 'fire all flaming,'[2]

[1] Gen. xix. 14. [2] 2 Thess. i. 8, 9.

Till the earth is all dissolved,[1]
Then they surely will remember
All the warnings and entreaties,
Which in love were given to them
By the men by God appointed.
  Such the thoughts which pressed upon them,
While they journeyed up the footpath
Of the steep and rugged mountain.
  As they turned their eyes where Sodom
Once was thronged with human beings,
They seemed carried o'er the chasm
Of four thousand years now by-gone,
To that morning—oh, how dreadful!
When the Lord in great displeasure,
'Rained on Sodom and Gomorrah
Fire and brimstone out of heaven,'[2]
When He overthrew those cities,
There destroying all the people,
Till the smoke of all the country
Rose as from a fiery furnace.
  Some, 'tis said, have seen the ruins
A few fathoms 'neath the waters,
Which flow over where stood Sodom,
To the southern extreme borders
Of those waters dead and bitter.
  Far away in that direction,
Edward and Eliza saw where
Once the strongholds of Engedi
Were a shelter for poor David,
When he, like the hunted partridge,
Fled from Saul who sought to slay him.
  There it was that with three thousand,
'Chosen out of all of Israel,'[3]
Saul was conquered by that mercy
Shown to him when David had him
In his power, yet did not kill him.

[1] 2 Peter iii.   [2] Gen. xix.   [3] 1 Sam. xxiv.

'Tis no wonder Saul was melted,
And with tears said, Thou art righteous,
Thou with good hast me rewarded,
Whereas I have sought to slay thee.[1]
  Oh! how blessed 'tis to conquer
All our enemies who hate us
With the power of loving-kindness.

  Over barren hill and mountains,
Where none dwell except to plunder,
Often catching sights of Jordan,
And they thought also of Pisgah,
Four long hours they hastened onward.
  Finally, they reached the Kedron,
Where its waters force their way through
A deep chasm wild and gloomy,
Looking as if some convulsion
There had rent the rock asunder.
  'Twas a scene not soon forgotten :—
Deeper, deeper yawned the chasm,
Higher, higher rose the rampart
O'er the road on which they travelled.
As the glorious sun was gilding
With its golden light the hill-tops,
Then upon them burst the convent,
Where for centuries the monks have
Lived like Mar Sabâ its founder.
  Weary, weary, cold, and hungry,
Oh! how glad each of the party
Would have felt had they been welcome
To the good cheer of that convent.
But their law forbids that women
E'er should cross their holy threshold.
  Then it was one of the ladies
Wrote these lines in indignation,
And the next day sent them to them,

[1] 1 Sam. xxix.

Asking that they each might read them,
And be led to heart-felt sorrow
For their cruelty to women;—
Pure and virtuous, lovely woman,
Who unless by man first ruined,
Lifts him to a higher level,
Makes him more refined and loving.

Ye Monks of Mar Sabâ,
  Who've built your walls so high,
You will not let poor woman in,
  Even tho' she starve and die.

Think you, ye're Christian men,
  Or followers of One,
Who loved poor woman when on earth,
  E'en Mary Magdalene.

Sure ye had mothers once,
  And sisters good and dear,
Then for their sakes, be kind, we pray,
  And give us shelter here.

The wind goes howling by,
  The rain is falling fast,
Will ye not hear our plaintive cry,
  And shield us from the blast?

Farewell, ye cruel monks,
  We will not stay to sue,
But o'er the waters we will tell
  Of Mar Sabâ and you.

The next morning with the sunlight
Dr. B. and Edward Payson,
Having left their wives behind them,
Visited the sacred convent,
Which, for fourteen hundred years,
Has afforded food and shelter
To the hermits who frequent it.
   There they saw the bones of thousands,
Who once dwelt within those grottoes,
Excavated in the rocky
Sides of that precipitous mountain.
   To the place where once the lion
Shared its den with its first hermit
They were taken, and to places
Far too numerous to mention.
   Glad were they to see the blackbirds,
Which come daily to the convent,
Cheerful, joyous, full of music,
Singing to the gloomy hermits
Of their lives of happy freedom.
   Were these men indeed converted,—
Did they truly love the Saviour,—
Had they listened to His message,
'Go and preach my blessed Gospel
In the highways and the hedges;
Tell them of the great salvation
Which I offer to them freely;'—
Had they heard these words of Jesus,—
Had they hearts that truly loved Him,
Would they shut themselves in convents,
Living lives so lost and selfish,
Never caring for the millions
Longing for the light of knowledge,
Dying for the bread of heaven?
How unlike our blessed Master,
He who mingled with the people,

Seeking daily to instruct them
In the ways of heavenly wisdom.
 Can it be they know the Saviour,
Have they heard His cry, "*Tis finished,*'
Have they looked to Him for pardon?
 Oh thou God! who knowest all things,
Show them Christ, if they've not known him,
As the all-sufficient Saviour,
Lead them forth to love and serve Him
In a world where they are needed
In thy service so important.

 Leaving Mar Sabâ most gladly,
Bethlehem claimed their attention,
As it has the thoughts of millions :—
Bethlehem, where first our Saviour,
He the mighty God incarnate,
Took upon Him human nature,
That He might taste human suffering,
And be tempted like as we are.
 Three hours' riding ever rising,—
Then they saw the place where pilgrims
From all nations often gather,
There to think and talk of Jesus.
 Bethlehem is on a hill-top,
Fifteen hundred feet it rises,
Just like steps for some great giant,
Up the hillside, steep and rugged.
 O'er the place which long tradition
Fixes as the spot where Jesus
Once was cradled in a manger
Rises now a pile of buildings,
Most imposing in appearance.
 Oh! how little like a stable!
Rather like some old cathedral
Is the Church of the Nativity,

Built by the Empress Helena
Fifteen hundred years now by-gone.
　From this church descends a passage
Leading to the sacred grottoes.
　Following this with lighted taper,
They approached the place with reverence
Where Jerome, one of the fathers,
Sleeps that sleep that knows no ending
Till the trump that wakes the righteous
Calls them joyful forth to meet Him.
　Near his tomb they found his study,—
Now a chapel, with an altar,—
On which there is seen a painting
Of the saint engaged in writing;—
At his feet a sleeping lion.
　There it was that sainted father
Without any doubt resided;—
There was oft engaged in writing
Truths which make his name immortal,—
And translated there the Bible.
　Thence to a great massive column
The monk led them while he told them
'Twas the place where lay the hundreds
Little children slain by Herod,
Who thus sought the life of Jesus.
　Finally they reached the 'stable,'
Where by many thorough scholars
'Tis believed was born the Saviour;—
Justin Martyr thus believes it,
Origen also confirms it.
　Fixed within the pavement solid
Was a slab of purest marble,
On which was inscribed in Latin,
'Here was Jesus born of Mary!'
Sixteen lamps are there kept burning.
　There they also saw the manger
Where 'tis thought that Christ was cradled.

Oh! what feelings pressed upon them
While in Bethlehem they tarried.
They of Christmas oft were thinking,—
Christmas in their native country,
With its carols all so joyous.
 There they felt how condescending
Was the mighty God incarnate,
For our sake to take our nature,
Thus become a 'Man of sorrows.'
 Blessed Jesus! we adore Thee
For Thy wondrous love and pity
To our race so lost and fallen.
 Having left the gloomy Convent,
Through the town their way they threaded,
Through the throngs with trinkets loaded
To the building on the summit,
Where now lives a missionary;—
To the roof upon his house-top,
Thither hastened all the pilgrims,
Eager there to see the prospect,
On all sides so grand and glorious.
 To the east they saw the mountains,
Where the shepherds were abiding;
O'er their flocks their watch were keeping,
When the angel came upon them,
Saying, 'I have brought good tidings
Of great joy to all the people,
For this day is born a Saviour
In the city called "of David;"
Go and find Him in the manger.'
There it was, that with the angel,
Suddenly a host from heaven,
Sounded forth their songs of praises,—
'Glory be to God the highest.'
 Up that slope once climbed the Magi,
From their distant home in Persia,
Guided by the star of Bethlehem.

Yonder are the fields where Boaz
By the youthful Ruth was followed.
   Thither once the prophet Samuel
Came to anoint the son of Jesse—
He the shepherd boy of Bethlehem,
To be king o'er all of Israel.
   From that cave in yon Adullam,
'Twas that David longed for water [1]
From yon well, the well of Bethlehem;
Yet when from that well 'twas brought him
By three daring, valiant warriors,
Not a drop of it he tasted.
   But they oftener thought of Jesus,
How He left His throne in heaven,
Made His cradle in a manger
There in Bethlehem before them.
   Ere they left they purchased relics
To remind them of their visit
To the birthplace of our Saviour.
   Half an hour brought them where Rachel,
She the loving wife of Jacob, [2]
Died while in the way to Ephrath,
Having given birth to Benjamin.
   Now is marked her place of burial
By a small and white square building
Solitary by the wayside.
   Having gathered there some flowers,
On they passed by Mar Elias,
Where the Greeks have now a convent,
Who pretend that there Elijah
Lay beneath a branching olive,
When he fled from wicked Jezebel.
   Passing this, they reached the valley
Where once David fought the Philistines, [3]
As the Lord had him commanded.

[1] 2 Sam. xxiii. 14, 15.   [2] Gen. xxxv. 16.
[3] 2 Sam. v.

THE JEWS' WAILING PLACE.

Friday is the day for wailing,
When the Jews in numbers gather
Where once stood the mighty temple,
And around its great foundations
Stand and weep for hours together.
   At the time appointed Edward,
With his D.D. friend from Brooklyn,
And their wives intent were gazing
On the touching scene presented.
   Half a hundred there were weeping,
Or at least expressing sorrow,
At the temple's desolation.
   Here the Jews have been permitted
By the supercilious Moslems
To approach the sacred precincts
Of the temple of their fathers.
   Thither totter many aged,
There also are seen the youthful.
Jewish maidens they saw kissing
Stones that stood in Solomon's temple.
   Would that they would weep the rather
At the guilt of their forefathers,
In their treatment of Messiah,
When the Headstone of the corner
They so cruelly rejected,
Killing Him by crucifixion.

   On the eighth day of December,
Edward, Ida, Michael started
For the burial-place of Abraham,
And of Isaac and of Jacob.
   Oft they wondered where the roadways
O'er which history says that Solomon
In his chariot rode to Ethan,
Fifty furlongs from Jerusalem,
To the pools all full of water.

Years two thousand and five hundred
Have brought with them many changes
Since those days when Israel flourished
'Neath the smile of her protector.
Now, alas! there's not a chariot
In the land where once were thousands.
Now her highways are but footpaths,—
All is marked by desolation.

   Grievous have been their transgressions,
And their punishment deservèd.
   When they reached the pools of Ethan,
Built by Solomon the mighty,
There they found them near as perfect
As when they were first constructed
To hold water for the city.
Three there are of size near equal,
Fifty feet in depth the largest,
And six hundred feet its length is.
Yet they only fed one city,
While the waters of salvation
Will supply a world that's thirsty.

   Pools of Ethan now are useless;
But the waters of salvation
Still they flow as fresh as ever.
   At the well of living waters
We may say that here a greater
Far than Solomon is standing.
He is saying, 'He that drinketh
Of the waters that I give him,
Ne'er shall thirst again—no, never.'
Have you really drunk the water
Which shall quench your thirst for ever?—
Jesus offers you it freely.

   Twelve miles southward still was Hebron,
Long and tedious was the journey.
Constantly they passed by ruins,

Speaking to them of the people
Who once dwelt upon those hill-tops,
Ere the curse of God was on them.

Finally, they reached the valley
Where the grapes of Eshcol flourish.
Still they found the hill-sides covered
With the thickly-growing vineyards,
Guarded by the towers built in them.

In that valley 'twas that Abraham,
And that Isaac, also Jacob,
Dwelt at times, and there were buried—
'Twas the place of their encampment.

In his tent there Abraham rested,
When to him there came an angel,
Sent by God from out of heaven,
To announce to him that Sodom
And Gomorrah soon must perish
For their wickedness so heinous.

Here in Hebron 'twas that Sarah
Died, and in a cave was buried—
Machpelah, the name 'twas called by.
There in after years Rebekah's,
Also Leah's, place of resting.

Just before the sun was setting
Edward and Eliza rested
In a house for them provided
By the order of good Michael.
Glad were they of such a shelter,
For their tents were left behind them.
There they prayed the God of Abraham,
And of Isaac and of Jacob,
For His blessing to rest on them.

The next morning was the Sabbath,
Bright and glorious—Oh! how lovely
Rose the sun that charming morning!

To the housetop, early, Edward

Stole away for his devotions.
There with many tears he pleaded
That the Angel of the Covenant—
He who once with Jacob wrestled,
Would deny him not a blessing,
But would strengthen him for service,
And that he might, with his partner,
Live for God and do His bidding.
 When they moved among the thousands
Who now dwell where once ruled David,
Oh! how little like a Sabbath—
No one there revered that day when
Jesus rose o'er death triumphant.
 When they reached the sacred building,
The Mosque door stood widely open.
Feigning ignorance, they entered,
Where the Jews and where the Christians
Are forbidden by the Moslems.
Soon a turbaned man came running,
Holding up his hands in terror,
Seizing on them, drove them backward
To the door which they had entered.
Like the Prince of Wales, they wished that
They'd a *firman* from the Sultan;
So they had to be contented
With the outside of the harem,
With its bevelled stones as massive
As those in the sacred temple.
Sad it is that Moslem tyrants
Should possess the place which Christians
Might with profit often visit.
In the afternoon a funeral
Of a Moslem youth they witnessed;—
'Twas a spectacle of sadness.
 Monday morning, they were sitting
'Neath the ancient oak of Mamre,

Underneath which some say Abraham
Pitched his tent when there he tarried—
Near a mile it is from Hebron.
This to them was very doubtful;
But they gathered from it branches
To remind them of their visit.
As they turned and looked on Hebron,
Which was once a refuge city,
Then they thought of the manslayer
Fleeing thither from the avenger,
Who would slay him if he lingered.
Oh! how much has changed that city
Since the Levites were its keepers!
 Twenty miles that day they travelled,
Each on horseback, to the city
Where the Root and where the Offspring
Of King David for us suffered.

 Tuesday morning they inspected
The old archway which supported
The grand causeway from the temple,
To the palace of King Solomon,
Situated on Mount Zion.[1]
Thence they turned, thro' a small gateway—
'Needle's Eye,' the name 'twas called by,
By the guide who them conducted.
Even through it might a camel
Pass, if left behind the panniers,
Which he almost always carries.
 Then they thought about the rich man,[2]
Who might pass the gate called Wicket,
If he thinks more of his Saviour
Than he does of all his riches.
 Thence into the Vale of Hinnom,
Where were burned their sons and daughters
As a sacrifice to Moloch,

 [1] 1 Chron. ix., and 1 Kings x.   [2] Matt. xix.

Which they made a hideous monster,
And within it placed a furnace.
There they in imagination
Saw the Hebrew mother standing
With her babe clasped to her bosom,
Gazing on it for the last time,
Ere 'twas cast into the red-hot
Arms of that dread fiery idol.
　Now 'tis for a place of burial.
And around its sides are tombstones,
As foretold by Jeremiah.[1]
　To the right the 'Field of blood' was,
Purchased by the gains of Judas,
For betraying Christ our Saviour.[2]
Leaving these they hastened down where
Jeremiah (says tradition)
By a cruel saw was sundered.
　Underneath frowning Moriah,
At the foot of mount called Ophel,
Where the Vale of Kedron joineth
With the valley—*Tyropeon*,—
There Siloam's sacred waters
Flow as in the days when Jesus
Bade the blind man wash within it.[3]
Long beside that pool they tarried,
Not as lovely as when by it
Were the cultivated gardens
Of the mighty King of Israel.
　Yet the fact that often Jesus
Had stood by those placid waters
Made them in their eyes attractive.
Thinking of those hallowed waters,
Edward wrote these lines about them:—

　　Within the Kedron's rocky dell,
　　　Beneath Moriah's frowning face,

[1] Jer. xix.　[2] Matt. xxvii.　[3] John ix.

THE POOL OF SILOAM.

Siloam's waters often tell
   Of Jesus' love and wondrous grace.

There softly flows Siloam's rill,
   As in the day Isaiah sang.
'Twas there the blind man's heart did thrill,
   While with his song the valley rang.

Siloam means, 'one sent from God,'
   Such is the lovely name it bears;—
It teaches that from His abode
   Are blessings that should banish cares.

Dear Saviour, like this sparkling spring,
   May we to others speak of Thee,
That they with us may also sing,
   See what the Lord hath done for me.

CHAPTER XVIII.

AT the fountain of the Virgin,
　In the valley of the Kedron,
　　There they saw the waters springing
From the side of rocky Ophel.
Bright and sparkling are its waters:
A tradition says, if women
Drink it who have lost their virtue,
Quick they die—by heaven smitten.
　When the virgin was accusèd
That she had not to her husband
Come a chaste and virtuous maiden,
She endurèd this ordeal,—
Thus was innocence established.
'Fountain of accusèd women,'
Was the name which it long went by.
Some suppose that all its waters
Flow from underneath the Haram,
'Neath the altar where the temple
Reared its lofty tower to heaven.
　Up a little farther northward,
Near the channel of the Kedron,
Is the tomb of Zecharias,
Who was stoned within the temple
In the reign of King Josiah.[1]
Near it is the tomb of Absalom,
With its lower part a mon'lith

[1] 2 Chron. xxiv. 21.　Matt. xxiii. 35.

Cut from out the solid mountain;
Every Jew that passeth by it
Throws a stone in detestation
Of his crime against King David.
   After seeing where the prophets
(So **tradition** says) **were** buried,
Having entered where their ashes
Long repose in solemn silence,—
Then with eager steps they hastened
To Gethsemane, where Jesus
Oft retired to pray in secret,
And where He, with His disciples,
On that fearful night of sorrow,
Prayed **till** bloody sweat fell from **Him**—
From His brow so marred with anguish.
Then they plucked some leaves from olives—
Olives, surely very agèd—
Some say, underneath which Jesus
Sweat those drops of blood in anguish;
Possibly their *roots* were moistened
With that blood, tho' other branches
May **have** taken since the places
Of those which **were** there when Jesus
Oft for prayer resorted thither.
   Ne'er will Edward and Eliza
Cease to thank their heavenly Father
For their visit to that Garden.
   With a heart with love o'erflowing,
Edward penned these lines impromptu:—

   My Jesus, I would ne'er forget
     That hour I spent with Thee;
   When there I saw Thy bloody sweat
     In dark Gethsemane.

'Twas in that olive press I felt
　　That Thou didst bleed for me;—
Alas! how great I saw my guilt
　　While in Gethsemane.

I thought of how Thy heart did throb,
　　While 'all' Thine own did flee,
And left Thee with the cruel mob
　　In sad Gethsemane.

How earnestly with tears we pled
　　For friends across the sea,
That they might cling to Thee who bled
　　In lone Gethsemane.

'Twas there I felt my guilt and shame
　　In oft forsaking Thee;
How precious was Thy very name
　　In dear Gethsemane.

Should e'er our love to Thee grow cold,
　　And we forgetful be,
We'll call to mind Thy love untold
　　While in Gethsemane.

CHAPTER XIX.

'NEATH the ramparts of the city,
Is the entrance to those caverns,
Which of late have been discovered,
And excited deepest interest.
Twice the travellers from America
Entered that mysterious region.
Torches in abundance made its
Chambers look like vast cathedrals;—
Rough they were, yet most majestic,
Like a row of Gothic churches
Stretch these subterraneous caverns,
Far away beneath the temple.
Oft they feared some lurking Bedwin
From his lair might spring upon them;
But from this they were protected.
Now you ask, what caused these caverns—
Were they made by man or nature?
Soon this question can be answered;—
For on every side were marks of
Implements of the stone-cutters
Who, in centuries now by-gone,
There had quarried stones most massive
For the building of the temple.
There they saw the little niches
Where the workmen's lamps had rested
While they patiently were cutting
Out the blocks for Sol'mon's temple.

They, perchance, that very morning
In the halls beneath el-Aksa,
Had beheld the stones that once were
Taken from those very caverns.
For beneath the Mosque of Omar
Is the shaft thro' which the stones were
Lifted to their place of resting
In that grand majestic structure
For the worship of Jehovah.
Then they understood that passage
In the Book of Kings,[1] which speaketh
Of the stones that were made ready
Ere they came into the temple,
So that not the sound of hammers
Once was heard when it was building.
Thus that statement in the Bible,
Which before had seemed mysterious,
Was interpreted most clearly.

Only underneath the temple,
In that place so dark and dreary,
Were the stones with many knockings
For the building smoothly polished—
Much like this God's plan of working
With the stones of His selecting,
For the temple which in heaven
He will rear for His own glory,
Built upon the sure foundation
Of the apostles and the prophets,—[2]
Jesus Christ our Saviour being
There, the chief stone of the corner.
God, in mercy grant that we may
Each have patience for the trials
That shall fit us for that temple
Where, as lively stones well polished,
We shall dwell with Him for ever.

[1] 1 Kings vi. 7. [2] Eph. ii. 20.

Lord, grant that we with faith may see
    Our new Jerusalem above,
Where we, from sin and sorrow free,
    Shall dwell with Thee where all is love.

A while we linger here below,
    Where oft it seems so dark and drear,
But soon to Zion's courts we'll go,
    Where none will ever shed a tear.

Then shall Jerusalem be ours,
    Where prophets and where martyrs dwell—
Then shall we pass the golden hours
    In joys that none on earth can tell.

Help us with patience, Lord, to bear
    The strokes of Thine afflicting rod;
As stones well polished by Thy care,
    May we in heaven grace Thine abode.

    In Jerusalem are children,
Near a hundred, who speak English,—
In the schools they've been instructed.
    These dear children, Bishop Gobat,
Bishop of the Church of England,
Brought together with some others
That they each might hear of Jesus
From the lips of Edward Payson,
Hoping that some word he uttered
Might be blessed by God's own Spirit.
    Oh! how strange it seemed to Edward

To be speaking of the Saviour
In the city where He suffered,
Urging all to trust and love Him.
Oh! how could they see the places
Where our dear Redeemer suffered,
And forget Him, yea, reject Him?
Yet the heart of man is human
In all ages, and all places,
And without the Spirit's power,
It will never love the Saviour.

    Judas daily saw his Master,
Saw the works He wrought so mighty,
Saw Him call the dead to being,
Heard His words so pure and holy,
Saw Him over sinners weeping,—
Heard Him preaching to them pardon,—
Yet this Judas never loved Him,
No, the rather he betrayed Him,
Led the cruel murd'rers to Him,—
Therefore 'tis not such a wonder
That there live in that same city
Those who still reject the Saviour.
Edward told them of the children
Many hundreds, even thousands,
Far away beyond the ocean,
Who had learned to trust in Jesus,
Who not far from where they then were
Suffered on the cross that children
Might be brought at last to heaven;
Bishop Gobat also urged them
Each to heed the kindly message,
And like children o'er the ocean,
Come at once and trust the Saviour.

    In the evening Mrs. Gobat
Kindly asked some friends to gather
At their house upon Mount Zion,

That their friends from o'er th' Atlantic
Might by them be kindly greeted.
Edward then received a present
From the hands of Mrs. Gobat,
Which to him is of more value
Than the richest gold of Ophir,—
I will tell you all about it.
　All around the Holy City,
Thorn trees grow in great abundance,
Bearing thorns like those which once were
Plaited in the crown which Jesus
Wore when in the house of Pilate.
From these bushes Mrs. Gobat
Kindly gathered thorns and wove them
In a crown like that our Saviour
Wore upon His brow with meekness.
　This she gave to Edward Payson,
To remind him of Christ's sufferings,
And that he might sometimes show it
To the youth and to the children
In the places where he laboured,
That the death of Christ the Saviour
Might appear to them more real.
　Early Wednesday morn they started
From Jerusalem for Jaffa,
Thirty days they'd been on horseback,
In November and December,
Which is called the rainy season,
Yet it only rained for three days,
Even then they did not tarry,
For they had their water-proofs on,
Which protected them entirely.
　Many were the weary pilgrims,
Whom they met all unprotected,
Even some from far-off Russia,
Toiling up and down those hill-sides,

Rocky, slippery, oh! how tedious,
On their way to see where Jesus
Gave Himself a willing off'ring
That He might redeem His people.

On their way, they crossed the brook where
David found that stone so deadly,
With which he once slew Goliath
On the day when the Philistines
Challenged all the hosts of Israel,
Asking them to meet their champion.

From that brook some stones they gathered,
'Smooth' and round like those which David
In his shepherd's bag collected,
When he cast aside Saul's armour,
And on God alone depended,
That the earth might know most surely,
That there was a God in Israel.

Finally, the rain clouds lifted
As they entered into Ramleh,
Glad they were for rest and shelter,
Even in the Latin Convent,
With its poor accommodation.

In the morning they made ready
To ascend the Campaneli,
The old hill tower which for centuries
Has o'erlooked the vale of Sharon,
For at least five hundred years.
Saracenic is its structure,
Like the old red tower of Halle.

From its top they looked on Lydda,
Only a short distance north-east,
Where once Peter cured Æneas,
Who for eight long years was palsied,
Then it was that all at Lydda,
And about the vale of Sharon,
When they heard it, turned to Jesus.[1]

[1] Acts ix. 35.

Oh! how glorious was the prospect
On that mild November morning
When upon the vale of Sharon,
From the sea to the dark mountains,
Played the shadows and the sunlight,—
Emblem of a life that's chequered,
With its joys and with its sorrows.

Soon they bid adieu to Ramleh,
And its minaret so lofty,
Where once stood the Mosque for Moslem,
And where many bold crusaders,
Following their valiant Richard,
Fiercely fought and fell while fighting
With the Moslems whom they hated,
And with Saladin their chieftain.

While upon their way to Jaffa,
They o'ertook a Russian Princess,
Who, because she loved the Saviour,
Left her children and her husband
In the capital of Russia,
And had travelled all that distance,
That she might behold those places
Rendered sacred by the Saviour,
When He lived on earth abasèd.

With her maid and with her brother,
She had been thro' Palestina—
To the birthplace of our Saviour,
To the garden where He suffered,—
Tho' a member of the Greek Church,
Yet with all its many errors,
In it she had heard of Jesus,
Of His dying love for sinners;
She had come to Him for pardon,
And in Him alone was resting
For salvation and for comfort.

Many trials she had suffered,

But her countenance was radiant
With the joy of sins forgiven,
And with ardent love for Jesus.
Many days they kept together,
Even till they came to Naples.
Crossing o'er the plains of Sharon,
Edward a gazelle spied flying
Like a deer across their pathway,
Then with Michael's gun he started
With his steed half-bred Arabian,
Like the wind he flew so quickly
That his Ida was affrighted
When she saw him in the distance.
Fast he gained, but soon he halted,
When he came to ground all marshy—
O'er it the gazelle skipped lightly,
But the horse was quickly floundered,
And perchance 'twas well it was so,
For E.'s heart would sure have failed him,
For so lovely and so gentle
Was the shy gazelle he hunted.

  As they nearer drew to Jaffa,
All at once they found that they were
In an orange-grove most lovely.

  Nowhere had they in their travels,
Seen the fruit so ripe and luscious,
Some were hanging o'er the road-side,
And so tempting that they plucked them,
And they found them most refreshing,
For altho' 'twas mid December,
Still they found the sun oppressive.

On the thirteenth of December,
Safely each one of the party
Reached the city now called Jaffa.
As they rode along the suburb,
Oh! how much were they delighted
With the orange groves so luscious.

Not alone their eyes were feasted,
But their hands were once uplifted,
As they rode along on horseback,
And they plucked the fruit so tempting,
Which within their mouth soon melted.

After lunch they turned their faces
To the house where 'Simon Peter'
Lodged with 'Simon,' called a 'tanner,'
And they went upon the housetop,
Where by God he was instructed
That among both Jews and Gentiles,
He who in the Saviour trusteth,
Should of sins receive remission.

They were much impressed to notice
That upon that very housetop,
Which tradition says was Simon's, (?)
There is now a brilliant lighthouse
Set to guide the nightly mariner
Past the rocky coasts of Joppa,
Where so many have been shipwrecked.

But a *truth* has been reflected
From that housetop since the day when
Peter saw the 'heaven opened,'
Which afar has penetrated
Wheresoe'er is preached the Gospel,
Showing God is no 'respecter'
Of the Jews more than of Gentiles,
But that all who fear and love Him
Will for Christ's sake be receivèd.

Vainly asked they many natives

For that ancient upper chamber
Where the widows stood by weeping,
Showing all the coats and garments,
Handiwork of sleeping Dorcas,
And where Peter came with power
From the mighty God of heaven,
Raising her from death so quickly,
That they all were much astonished,
So that thro' the town of Joppa
Many in the Lord believèd—
Sure enough the monks will take you
To a place they have invented
As the very house of Dorcas,—
All they care for is the money,
Which they get from passing travellers.

But they knew they were in Joppa,
Hallowed with associations.

From that city 'twas that Jonah
From the presence of Jehovah
Hasted in a ship to Tarshish.

Thither also from Mount Lebanon
Came the cedars for the temple.

The next day on board the 'Volga'
They embarked for Alexandria.
Sad were they to part with Michael,
Who had ever been so faithful
During all their Syrian journey.
Sadder still to leave that country,
Where so long they had been wandering,
And experienced such enjoyment.
While the ship lay in the harbour,
Long delaying its departure,
On that bright and sunny morning
Edward's thoughts were ever lingering
Round the scenes with which he'd parted—
In these lines he thus expressed them:—

FAREWELL TO PALESTINE.

Thou Holy Land, adieu!
    Farewell ye Bible scenes;
Soon thou wilt vanish from our view,
    Thou Land of Palestine.

From thee the Saviour rose
    Victorious o'er the grave,
Thus triumphing o'er all His foes,
    That He the lost might save.

'Twas from thine Olive Mount
    He left the sight of men,
And on that mount His feet shall stand
    When He shall come again.

We thank our blessed Lord
    That we have seen thy face,
With more of love we'll read His Word,
    And thus its beauty trace.

We've climbed thy rugged hills,
    And scaled thy mountains high;
We've rested by thy sparkling rills,
    But now a long good-bye!

    After forty hours of sailing
O'er the classic Mediterranean,
It was on a Lord's-day morning
That they landed in the city
Built by the great Alexander.
    With the help of Captain Layard
They passed thro' the ranks of Arabs,

Who like harpies thronged around them,
Always crying, 'Backshish, Backshish.'
  Soon within the house of worship,
With an English congregation,
They were praising God their Father
For His many, many mercies.
  There they thought of bold Apollos,
Mighty in the Holy Scriptures,
Who was born in that same city.
Also thought of Mark the apostle,
Who once preached in Alexandria,
And how he there died a martyr,
Dragged with fury thro' the city,
All because he preached so plainly,
Warning men of their destruction,
If in sins they still persisted,
And the love of Christ rejected.
  There they found a train for Cairo,
Into which they gladly entered.
  Soon along Lake Mareotis
They were hastening to the river
Which converts the gloomy desert
Into a rich blooming garden.
  They first saw the branch Rosetta
Spanned with a strong bridge of iron.
Thence they journeyed on to Delta,
To the branch called Damietta,
Passing fields of snow-white cotton.
Tho' it was in mid December,
It was like the hottest weather
Of new England in midsummer.
  There they saw the ox and camel
Ploughing side by side together,
Also saw the tamèd bison
Patient turning up the furrows.
Everywhere amongst the green fields

Met their eyes the sacred Ibis,
Long since worshipped by the Egyptians.
   One they saw light on a bison,
Tame and white—it was so beauteous
That they could not help admire it,
But they still were sad to think that
Men should worship earthly creatures
Rather than the great Creator.
   Ancient Cairo ! ah ! how strangely
Looked that old Egyptian city.
There they saw from every nation
Blacks and whites all mixed together,
Moslem women with veiled faces,
Slaves to men of brutal passions,
Who have never learned the lesson
That the woman is man's equal—
Never made to be a plaything,
But the rather a true helpmeet,
Ne'er dividing his affections
With another wife or lover,
But absorbing them entirely,
Thus, and only thus made happy.
   Soon they mounted on some donkeys,
And away they quick were driven
To the Citadel of Mahomet,
Of the great Mahomet Ali.
   It of all the Mosques they'd entered,
With its alabaster columns,
Was by far the very finest,
Not excepting Mosque of Omar,
Nor the great Mosque of Damascus.
   In one corner they were pointed
To Mahomet Ali's Tombus,
Tho' the building was in honour
Of Mahomet Ali's genius,
Still the castle close adjoining,

Where he slaughtered all the Mam'lukes,
Except one who, on his charger,
Leaped with fury o'er the precipice,
Far down on the rocky pavement,
Killing quick his noble war-horse,
Is a relic of his cruelty.

But the view from that high eminence
Was of most surpassing beauty,—
Pyramids, tho' ten miles distant,
Seemed but just across the river.
Neither did they look so large as
The great monuments they'd read of.
They in number count some fifteen
At Sakkarah and at Shireh.

The next morning they were early
On their saddles for the Pyramids.
Signor Fenzi with his daughters
Very kindly joined their party.

Three miles riding down to Boulah,
Underneath the branching sycamores,
And the tall and stately palm trees,
Brought them to the part of Cairo
Where a boat was ready waiting
To conduct them o'er the river,
O'er the wondrous 'King of Rivers,'
Which converts the sandy desert
Into rich and verdant gardens.

On they hastened to the Pyramids,
Thro' the fields all green and verdant.

Oh! how hard it was to realize
That it was in mid December,
Rather was it like a May day
On the banks of Susquehanna.

Some were gathering in the harvest,
Indian corn was ripe and yellow,
Others cutting down the clover.

Passing on they reached the desert,
On whose border stand those monuments,
Which long since were seen by Moses,
And by Abraham when in Egypt,
Yes, by Jeremiah even
When in Egypt he was captive,—
Also by Napoleon Bonaparte,
At the battle of the Pyramids,
When to stimulate his warriors,
He repeated words so memorable,
Making them a magic watchword,
'Soldiers! brave men—each remember
There are looking down upon you
Memories of years four thousand.'
    When at length the eager pilgrims
Stood beside the massive Pyramids,
Oh! how different seemed their aspect
From their appearance in the distance.
    Cheops claimed their first attention,
Covering at least twelve acres,
Towering, oh! how high toward heaven.
    Then arose th' important question,
Who'll ascend the topmost summit,
O'er those steps three feet in thickness?
Signorina, Maid of Florence,
Quickly said, Yes, I will do it;
Ida, from the Susquehanna,
Full of zeal, said, I will do it.
    Edward thus was much delighted
With his wife so energetic,
Who was ready to go with him
To the top of giant Cheops.

When the two to ascend had once made the decree,
Then the Arabs were gathered as thick as could be,
All were ready and anxious to lend them their aid,
Upon the condition that they were well paid.

To describe then what followed would puzzle, I wot,
Lytton Bulwer or Dickens or Sir Walter Scott,
You'd have laughed to have seen how they laid hold the wife,
How they dragged her away from her partner for life.

Each one held her as if she belonged all to him,
Just as if for her husband they cared not a pin,
With a leap and a jump they each pulled her along,
And they sought to allay all her fears with a song.

When her husband all breathless once flew to her aid,
She then quickly cried out, 'Oh! dear, no, I'm afraid;
These wild Arabs are strong, much stronger than you,
Surely this is the work they know well how to do.'

When at length they had planted their feet on the top,
All their fears and their sorrows were quickly forgot;
On every side there were sights to behold,
But alas! by this pen they can never be told.

Far away to their right was where Memphis once dwelt,
That city whose power o'er all Egypt was felt,

Where Pharaoh once ruled, and where Moses was
    reared,
And where he returned with a power to be feared.

Heliopolis, which in the Bible is On,
And where all the people once worshipped the sun,
Lay there full in view, but a few miles away,
But oh! where's its glory? alas! none can say.

It was in that same city that Plato once taught,
And there it was also Herodotus wrought,
But now thousands of years have flown by since that
    day,
And its temples and grandeur have gone to decay.

And from thence it was too that God's chosen race
Fled away quick in haste from King Pharaoh's face;
When the Lord, with a high and an uplifted hand,
Led them forth on their journey to the promised land.

When our Saviour hung bleeding on sad Calvary,
And the sun was refusing the dread sight to see,
Then the darkness which covered the great Sacrifice,
It was seen then in On, by astronomers' eyes.

Far away in the distance they also could see,
What their dragoman told them was the very tree,
Where the Virgin with Jesus an infant sat down,
When they fled where by Herod they could not be
    found.

And there was the river which flows just the same
As when Moses an infant upon it was lain;
Mighty cities that rose from its banks in their pride,
They have crumbled to dust, but there still flows the tide.

All majestic the Sphinx rose from out of the sand,
As if guarding the mummies from some ruthless hand,
Which for ages has looked on the vale of the Nile,
On its joys and its sorrows, nor wept once nor smiled.

But the sight which amazed them the most in that plain,
Which they looked at with wonder again and again,
Was the great Pyramid tow'ring high in the air,
And to climb to the top was their hardest task there.

CHAPTER XX.

BUT we must not stop to speak of
All the pilgrims saw in Egypt.
Sure, of all the many places
They had been to in their wanderings
It to them was the most novel;
Nowhere were its crowds so motley,
As along the flowing waters
Of the mighty king of rivers.

But their friends seemed often beckoning,
Saying, loved ones, hasten homeward,—
Come and buckle on the harness,
Which you now have long been free from.

To the call they were obedient,—
Thus upon the Mediterranean
They set sail upon a steamer,
Bound for Sicily and Naples.

All went well till the third morning,
When a gale from Adriatic,
Such a one as Paul encountered,
Fourteen days and nights in Adria,
Threatened to engulf their vessel.
They like him were forced to linger
Under Crete against Salmone.

There for hours full eight and forty,
They were tossed upon its waters,
Altho' sheltered by the mountain,
Lofty snow-capped—how majestic.

After many prayers were offered,
Finally, the wind abated;
And they sailed along Achaia,
Wishing much to land at Athens,
But the land that first appeared
Was Mount Etna—oh! how glorious,
Robed with snow two miles in air,
Sleeping like some mighty giant,
All unconscious of its power
To belch forth its liquid fire
With reverberating thunder,
From its vast and lofty crater,
Making all the island tremble,
As if in the Day of Judgment.

Finally, their ship dropped anchor
In Messina's lovely harbour
On a charming Christmas morning,
When the bright flags all were flying
In the bay and in the city.

Then they drove to Telegraph Mountain,
Up two thousand feet its level,
Above Scylla and Charybdis,
Seen so plainly from its summit.

Right before them was Stromboli,
Which once rose from out the water,
Casting up its liquid lava
Till it formed a mighty mountain,—
Oh, how wonderful its aspect!
Boiling still with molten lava.

There was also the Mount Vulcan,
With his vast and heated workshop:—
One would think the flood of water
All around would quench his fires,
Thus destroying his employment,
But he never borrows trouble,
Tho' the waters roar above him,

Seeking oft to gain admission
To his subterranean chambers.
 On their right lay peaceful Rhegium,[1]
Where Paul tarried when he hastened
Toward his landing at Puteoli.
 Oh! how genial was the climate,
And the air—oh, how luxurious!
Bearing on its bosom fragrance
From the orange groves so luscious.
 Finally, their visit ended,
They took steamer bound for Naples.
 In avoiding rocky Scylla,
Like to many navigators,
They were not so very cautious
As to run into Charybdis,
But they took the course that's medium,
Thus escaping both the dangers
Of the sunken rocks and whirlpool.
 Thus they prayed that in life's voyage,
They might ever more be guarded
From extremes that are so dangerous,
From each Scylla and Charybdis.
 After sailing past Calabria,
Gazing oft upon its castles,
Calling up the classic stories,
Thrilling tales of days now by-gone,—
Finally, they neared Vesuvius,
And the charming Bay of Naples.
 Many days they spent in visiting
All the objects of deep interest,
Which were everywhere so numerous.
 In the museum they lingered,
Where they found so many relics
From the city of Pompeii,
And the buried Herculaneum.
 There they saw the bread the baker

---

[1] Acts xxviii.

Had made ready for the oven,
With his name all stamped upon it.
   Little did the maker think then
That the bread he there was making
Would be baked with fire Volcanic,
And be covered with its scoriæ
Seventeen hundred years and over,
And be gazed upon by thousands,
Who would come from distant countries
To the excavated city.
   There they learned what were the customs
Of the ancient Roman people
In the days when the arts flourished,
Which have been the admiration
Of all ages since that period.
   Often there they were attracted
By the jewels and the bracelets
Found on bones which once were covered
With the flesh of Pompeii's daughters.
   There the stocks in which the prisoners
Were held fast when the Volcano
Belched forth liquid fire and ashes,
Were before them all as perfect
As tho' they had not been buried
More than seventeen hundred years.
   If they only could have spoken,
What a tale of grief and sorrow
Would they tell about the victims
They enchained when many hundreds
Fled away from their embraces.
   Beautiful Mosaic tables,
Once the pride of gay patricians,
Candelabras, unique patterns,
Found with many other bronzes,
Marble statues full of beauty,
Long since chiselled by the sculptors

Celebrated among artists.
These and many other objects
Interested much the travellers.
   With the train one morn they started
Down to see the famed Pompeii,
Which was once the home of many
Who, without one hour's warning,
Were destroyed by the eruption
In the year of nine-and-seventy.
   Oh! how silent and how solemn
Seemed that city to the travellers.
There they saw the very houses,
Yea, the rooms in which were gathered
Feasting parties when the warnings
From Jehovah quickly called them
Each to leave his sins and pleasures,
And to hear the solemn verdict
From the judgment-seat of heaven.
In these rooms were found their bodies,
Each one seemed as if embalmed
With Egyptian magic power.
   In one room a greedy miser,
With his treasures, was uncovered.
Close beside him was a basket
Made of wire all wove together,
In which were three hundred pieces—
Some of gold, the rest of silver.
   He with others saw the danger,
Heard the rumbling of the mountain,
Saw it pouring forth the lava,
Felt the air all full of cinders,
Heard the people rushing past him,
Fleeing to a place of safety,
Heard the earnest warnings to him,
Bidding him no longer tarry
To secure his paltry treasures.

But, alas! he loved his money
Far too well to heed their caveats.
While he, therefore, there was gathering
Eagerly his loved possessions,
Down upon him came the scoriæ
In such masses that it buried
Him alive with all his riches.

   What a warning he to sinners
Who have heard Mount Sinai's thunders,
Been awakened to their danger,
And been told of Christ their Refuge,
Who is waiting to receive them,
And to shield them from destruction,
But who, for forbidden pleasures,
On the brink of ruin linger.

   As they walked about the city,
Looking at its charming villas,
At the temples of their deities,
Saw the worship paid to Venus—
Saw the frescoes in the houses—
Pictures oft too vile to mention,—
It was then they ceased to wonder
That the jealous God of heaven
For their sins, like unto Sodom,
Rained upon them fire and brimstone.

   They were also much astonished
With the things at Herculaneum,
Buried deep beneath the surface,
With the hard and solid lava,
Which, like an invading army,
With a power that nought could vanquish,
Crushed and overwhelmed the city.

   There they saw the massive theatre,
Seating full ten thousand people,
Many feet beneath the surface.

   After having seen the cities,

ASCENT OF VESUVIUS.

They, of course, were very anxious
To ascend that wondrous mountain,
Whence had flowed those streams of lava
Which had covered up the cities
Which were lying 'neath its shadow.

This they did, but who can narrate
What they saw upon that mountain?
'Twas a sight that should be witnessed,
For no pen could e'er describe it.
No one could forget his feelings
While he gazed into the crater,
For the fires of earth the chimney,
Whence escape the smoking gases
Of the furnace at its centre.

On all sides the view was glorious.
Castle Amare and Lorento,
Capria and all the islands,
Basking in the Bay of Naples,
Formed a scene not soon forgotten.

One day on their way to Baiæ,
They stopped at the tomb of Virgil,
Near by where 'tis said his house stood.
Now a simple modern tombstone,
Underneath a small stone archway,
Marks the place of his last resting,
Till the trump that wakes creation
Sounds to summon all to judgment.

On they passed thro' the long tunnel,
Which was cut clear thro' the mountain.
There it was when the Apostle,
The Apostle to the Gentiles,
Landed near at Puteoli.

Thither to that place they hastened;
But tho' Paul there left his footprints,
They of them could find no traces.
But they found the Egyptian Temple,

Which for several hundred years
Was submerged beneath the ocean.
   Not far off the Amphitheatre,
Where once fought the gladiators—
Yes, where once the cruel Nero
Stood himself in the arena.
   Soon they stood by Lake Averno,
Spoken of in classic history,
Near which was the Sybil's grotto,
Fabled place for revelations,
To which many oft resorted
When their way was dark and dubious.
   Where once stood the ancient temple,
Now, alas! are heaps of lava
Covering o'er the gorgeous temple,
With its wealth and all its grandeur.
   Thence to Baiæ they were driven,
Where the Romans spent their summers,
Bathing in domains of Neptune,
Where oft came the chaste and virtuous,
Like Penelope, the Grecian,
Who, like Helen, oft were ruined
By some villain like to Paris.
   There the Temple of Diana
Stands majestic in its ruins.
Many other nameless structures
Speak the wealth of lovely Baiæ,
When proud Rome was in her glory.
   Near Missinim they were pointed
To the fields they call Elysium,
Often named in classic history.
   While returning they were taken
To the ancient baths of Nero,
Boiling hot from 'neath the lava—
Yes, so hot that in three minutes
Eggs were nicely boiled within it.

Like a furnace was the passage
Which conducted to the Thermae,
Showing that the fires interior
Near approached unto the surface,
Warning all of constant danger.
   But their time was not all taken
Up with seeing sights in Naples.
Often Edward met the children,
Speaking to them of the Saviour,—
Of His wondrous love in dying
For them on the cross of Calvary,
That their sins might be forgiven.
Some of those Italian children
Seemed to understand the message,
And a few at least 'twas certain
Gave themselves up to the Saviour,
Trusting in the one great Offering.
Day by day were hundreds gathered,
That they thus might hear of Jesus.
   Oh! how tender were their feelings
When they heard the simple story—
Of the Saviour's sufferings for them.
   Finally, for Rome they started,
Once the capital of nations,
Making laws for all the people,
Ruling with a hand of iron
Lands far distant from their city.
   On their way they passed thro' Capua,
Where the Carthagenian General,
Hannibal, the mighty warrior,
Led the people to revolt from
Roman power and Rome's protection,
Telling them that they could conquer
Rome, the capital of Italy.
But ere long the Roman generals,
With their mighty legions mustered

At the gates of Capua, asking
That they should at once surrender,—
For them there was no escaping.
Senators—yes, more than fifty—
One by one were there beheaded,
And the rest reduced to slavery
For their treason and rebellion
Against Rome, the queen of nations.

  Oh! how could they then help thinking
How thus sinners oft are taken
With the cunning craft of Satan,
Who, with lies full oft repeated,
Tells them that there is no danger
In rebelling from Jehovah.

  But how great will be their terror
In the awful Day of Judgment,
When they hear the fearful sentence—
'Ye are leagued with Satan's kingdom;
With him now you must be punished
In the prison house of justice,
There to dwell, yes, there for ever.'

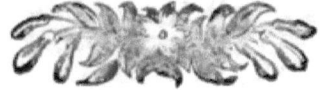

CHAPTER XXI.

MANY days in Rome they tarried,
Seeing all its sights and wonders;
Day by day they saw St. Peter's,
Gazed upon its dome so lofty,
Than the pantheon, much larger,
Handiwork of Michael Angelo.
   Every day the church seemed larger,
Till at last they were quite ready
To believe the fact that fifty
Thousand could be stationed in it,
And that it was more expensive
Than the churches of New England—
That it even cost more money
In its structure than the churches
Of those states all put together.
   God in mercy haste the day when
In it shall be heard the gospel,
Even as St. Peter preached it
On the day when full three thousand
Were converted, by the Spirit
Sending home the words he uttered.
   Raphael's 'Transfiguration,'
Prince of pictures, there they saw it
In the Vatican, where painters
From all nations flock to see it,
And for hours there gaze upon it.
   Then they saw all in Mosaic

The betrayal of our Saviour,
When by Judas in the garden
By a kiss he was delivered
To the death of crucifixion.
What a fiendish look had Judas!
   In the prison where tradition
Says St. Paul was once imprisoned,
(Mamertine, the name 'tis called by,)
There the pilgrims stood and listened
To the massive stones, which seemed to
Speak of how much Paul once suffered,
Waiting for his execution.
   There they saw the massive pillar
To which he by chains was fastened,
And the spring of purest water,
Which the monks with credence told them
God in mercy sent the apostles
When they there by cruel Nero
Were imprisoned, all because that
They would not deny their Saviour.
   Edward also saw the place where
Paul, 'tis said, was once beheaded.
Near that spot now is erected
A cathedral most majestic.
   In the Catacombs they wandered,
Thinking of those persecutions
Which once drove the Christians to them,
Forcing them to live in darkness
Rather than deny their Master.
Darkness?—no, the light of heaven
Shone effulgently upon them!
Yes, they had been brought from darkness
Into light that is most marv'llous.
   In those catacombs the bones are
Of the early Christians resting.
There '*in pace*' they will rest till

Jesus at the resurrection
Comes to gather all His people,
And redeem them from corruption.
Deeply were they interested
In deciphering the inscriptions
On the tombs of those dear Christians,
Who in Rome were persecuted,—
Each expressive of their faith in
Jesus as their Resurrection,
Who at last would change their bodies,
Causing them each to resemble
His own risen glorious body.
And with Christ they in the judgment
Will upon their persecutors
Speak the sentence that shall ever
Shut them in the pit of darkness,
Where no ray of hope shall enter.

   They within the Sistine Chapel
Saw that magnate *Pio Nono*
With his cardinals surrounded;
Saw them with profound submission
Kiss his toe with veneration;
Saw them bowing all before him,
As a solemn act of worship,
As if he were God from heaven.[1]

   They (no wonder) were disgusted
With the foolish genuflexions
Witnessed in the Sistine Chapel.

   On the spot where once the Cæsars
Lived within a golden palace,
Are extensive excavations.
These the pilgrims close inspected;
Saw the workmen there exhuming
Treasures which have lain for ages
Waiting for some antiquarian

[1] 2 Thess. ii. 4.

Who should bring them forth to tell us
Something more of Roman history,—
There they saw the richest vases—
Marble statues, which for ages
Have been buried and forgotten.
   'Twas for Ida's sake that Edward
Visited the city Roma.
It afforded him much pleasure
To point out to her the places
Which he had with much care studied
On a previous visit thither.
   Fourteen days they stopped in Florence—
Truly they were days of gladness—
There old friendships were rekindled;
Yes, and new ones too were lighted.
   There they gathered many children,
And they told them of the Saviour,
How He lovèd little children—
How He died that they might love Him,
That their sins might be forgiven.
Many wept to hear the story
Of His bloody sweat and passion
To secure the guilty, pardon.
Some of those dear children, also,
Truly seemed to trust in Jesus
As *their* Saviour, and to love Him.
They with these were more delighted
Than with all the sights of Florence.
Oft they saw the speaking marble,
From the sculptor's magic chisel;
But the sight of one 'new creature,'[1]
Fashioned into Jesus' image,
Fitted for those heavenly mansions,[2]
Was to them far more attractive
Than the finest marble statue.

      [1] 2 Cor. v. 17.   [2] John xiv.

Passing on thro' many cities,
Finally they came to Turin,
Where before them rose in splendour,
Alps on Alps, in solemn grandeur,
Like a massive wall of marble.
  Up those lofty Alpine mountains
They ascended by Mount Cœnis.
Words descriptive of such scenery
Are so often used in painting
Scenes of less imposing grandeur,
That they seem to lose their meaning.
Few can understand what feelings
Fill the soul on such occasions,
Unless they have climbed up mountains
Covered o'er with snow in summer.
They a sleigh-ride had in crossing
There among the snows eternal.
  Oft they prayed, that like those white peaks
They might live above poor worldlings,
Lives of purity and virtue,
And that like those snowy mountains,
When the sun upon them rises,
They might water those around them,
Filling many hearts with gladness.
  On thro' Switzerland they hastened,
Catching glimpses of its prospects—
On and on thro' France to Paris;—
There they lingered for a season,
While they held some children's meetings.
Much the children were affected
When they saw those thorns so cruel,
Which to E. had been presented
In that city where once Jesus
Wore a crown of thorns just like them
Till His brow was torn and bleeding.

Some among them seemed to feel that
'Twas for their sakes Christ was wounded,
That from sin they might be cleansèd.
    After one short week in Paris,
Then across the English Channel,
And to London, thence to Scotland,
With a day at Edinburgh,
Finally they stopped at Glasgow
With their friends, who kindly offered
Them a home and all they needed.
    But one day they left for Annan,
That dear place where Edward Payson,
With the Spirit's demonstration,
Preached till many hundreds heeded
The glad tidings of salvation.
    Pleasant was it after six years
To return and see those converts,
And to find them persevering
In the service of their Master.
    Then in Wales and parts of England
Edward and his helpmeet laboured,
Holding meetings long protracted,
Seeking to win souls to Jesus.
God stood by them in their trials—
Gave His Spirit to assist them,
So that many were converted
From their ways so full of error—
Yes, were turned to love the Saviour.
    Oxford was one of the places
Which they came to in their wanderings,
There they met with Dr. Pusey,
Who would make the Church of England
But the tool of Pio Nono;
God forgive him for the error
He hath everywhere been sowing.

THE THREE MARTYRS.

Strange it seemed that from that city
Where once Cranmer, and where Ridley
And where Latimer, were martyred,
Rather than deny their Saviour,
Even from that self-same city
Should go forth the very teachings
Which those martyrs so much hated.
   But among the many students
Some they found who loved the Saviour,
And were earnest in their efforts
To win others from their wanderings.
   Pleasant was their drive to Blenheim
Where Sir Walter often lingered—
Where he wrote his book called *Woodstock*.
   They from Oxford came to London
Only for a day to tarry,
But a friend whom they love dearly
Took them to his home directly;
Treated them just like his children—
Threw his heart into their life-work.
   His good wife was also with him,
In her kindness to the strangers—
For her heart was warm and tender—
She loved all who love the Saviour.
In that quarter they resided
Where once Watts, the sacred poet,
Went to pay a friend a visit
For two weeks or so—no longer,—
Yet full twenty years lived with him.
   E. and Ida sometimes wondered
If their hosts were not related
To the host of Watts, the poet.
Certainly they had his spirit,
For they made the strangers welcome,
Not for weeks but months the rather—

Sure the Lord, He will reward them
For their kindness to His servants,
For 'tis written,[1] 'He that giveth
Even but a cup of water
To a follower of Jesus,
Shall most surely be rewarded.'

Many pages might be written
Speaking of the work in London,
Which for months was carried forward
With the aid of God's own Spirit.

God be praised for all His goodness,
For the many joyous hundreds
Who were led to trust in Jesus.
'Twas His work—His be the glory.

Many were the noble workers
Who assisted oft in speaking
With the anxious, seeking Jesus,
Reverend Baptist Noel foremost,
Fearless in his Master's service,
Always happy with the children,
Teaching them to trust in Jesus.
Time would fail to speak of others,
Clergy, ministers, and laymen,
Who assisted Edward Payson
During his long stay in London,—
They in heaven will meet together,
And will join in Jesus' praises.

Now, my reader, have you followed
These two travellers in their journey?
Surely then you love the Saviour,
And though you may never wander
In the Via Dolorosa,
Where for us the cross He carried—
Tho' you ne'er may see the city

[1] Mark ix. 41.

Where for us He made atonement,
Yet if you are trusting Jesus—
Trusting only in His merits,
Then in raiment pure and spotless,
You within the holy city,[1]
With the saints and with the martyrs,
Shall be led to living fountains
By the Lamb who hath redeemed us.[2]
Even now God's Word believing,
You may sing with exultation:—

Thou hast taught us, dear Jesus, to look for the day
When the trumpet shall sound that shall call us away,
And when those who have died in the faith shall arise,
And with us who remain be 'caught up' to the skies.[3]

'Behold, quickly I come,'[4] were Thy words long ago,
But, oh! why, tell us why, is Thy progress so slow?
Oh! how many have watched, and have waited in vain,
And have died without seeing Thee coming again.

Well we know, blessed Lord, though Thy journey seems long—
Thou art hastening the day, when with one joyful song,
We shall hail thine appearing with sweet songs of praise,
And for ever shall dwell with the 'Ancient of days.'

[1] Rev. xxi. 2. [2] Rev. vii. 17. [3] 1 Thess. iv. 17.
[4] Rev. xxii. 12.

O Lord! we would stand with our lamps burning bright,
For Thy Word doth declare that far spent is the night;
Therefore, till Thou shalt come we will cling to that Word,
And be [1]'like unto men that do wait for their Lord.'

[1] Luke xii. 36.